Irresistible Italy

Irresistible *Italy*

A journey of the senses

Bill & Patsy Rowe

NH

NEW
HOLLAND

Acknowledgments

There are always so many people to say a special thank you to—I want to start by saying how grateful we are to Alvina and Umberto for their wonderful introduction to the world of the locals, the expats and above all, to life in the Italian countryside. To Markus Holzinger and Robyn Vulinovich for our magical stay at Villa Branca. And my fabulous students in our Tuscan Writer's Retreat: Pam Bradley, Louise Brazenor, Clare Clarke, Claire Darby, Nerida Melville-Smith, Vicki Ponsford, (will we ever forget those wondrous dinners?) and David Tieck, whose navigational and texting skills meant we found most places—most of the time.

I want to thank not only my students for their wonderful generosity in sharing their photographs with us when their shots were better than ours, but also Karin Cox, Michael Koukoudakis, Tiffany Johnson, Tony and Cheryl Medland, Pam Rushby and Janelle Ward for their fabulous shots. Thanks also to Mike Read, from Seggiano Produce, and dear friends from other wonderful trips: from David Lowe's Artists and Sculptor's group, the Corfields, Fearnsides, Ros Firth and our guide Dante Ghelfi. From the Dante Alighieri Language and Cultural Tour Giovanna Santomauro, Carlo Zincone and the Konigsbergs. A big thank you to Rita Pelliccia for her wonderful Torta d'erbi and to Anna La Torraca for her delicious recipes.

I would also like to thank one of the most imaginative and dynamic women in publishing today, Fiona Shultz, for asking us to write this book—which like most books I write, grew like topsy and seemed to take on a life of its own. Bill and I have had many wonderful trips to Italy and to have this book as a record of them is something we will always treasure. And finally, thanks to the publishing team, Lliane Clarke, Tania Gomes and Martin Ford at New Holland Publishers for their tremendous enthusiasm and above all, for their friendship.

ITALY

Verona

Venice

Portofino

Florence

Villa Branca
Mercatale

Cinque
Terre

Siena

Podere Nuovo
Castel del Piano

Grosseto

Rome

Naples

Sorrento

Positano

Adriatic Sea

Tyrrhenian Sea

Lipari Island

Sicily

Contents

The Menu
La Carta

Antipasto

Bruschetta with tomato and basil	21
Grissini	35
Asparagus with pecorino and pancetta	88
Tomato, bocconcini and basil salad	106

Pane—Bread

Oil for dipping:	
Lemon oil, Garlic oil, Pinzimonio	54
Tuscan sage and olive bread	62
Mushroom ciabatta	64

Torta e Frittata—Tarts

Torta d'erbe	57
Mediterranean tomato and cheese tarts	71
Frittata with	
roast pumpkin, potato and rosemary	100

Zuppa—Soup

Minestrone	58
Tomato and calamari soup	75
Chestnut soup	82
Tuscan bean soup	97

Pasta and Risotto

Alvina's walnut pesto pasta	44
Spinach and ricotta cannelloni	
with tomato sauce	48
Penne with herbs and parmesan	79
Risotto with	
baby spinach and gorgonzola	102
Mussels in white wine with spaghetti	122
Seafood tagliatelle	150
Pork and sage ravioli	160
Pasta al ragu	162

Pizza

Basic pizza dough	67
Artichoke, mozzarella and salami pizza	67

Piatto Principale—Main Course

Vitello—Veal

Saltimbocca alla Romana	22
Veal rolls with celery and gorgonzola	74
Rack of veal with	
thyme on garlic mashed potato	75

Introduction
All roads lead to Rome...

My love affair with Italy began when I was fourteen years old. My father was learning Italian at night school, purely as a hobby, and every evening as his homework spread out before him on the kitchen table, I would pore over his books, rolling my rrr's and begging to be allowed to go with him. Finally, he relented. From that day on, Italy became my obsession, as did my tutor's three handsome, lusty Italian sons: Sergio, Sandro and Silvio. I quickly ingratiated myself with all three, although their father preferred me to spend time with the fourteen-year-old daughter of the family, Stefania, so that I could help her learn English.

Like many Italian females, Stefania was olive-skinned and blessed with a flowing mane of dark hair, luminous brown eyes that hinted at secrets a fourteen-year-old shouldn't know, and a voluptuousness that belied her youth. In contrast, I was petite, pale, blonde and flat-chested. I had no secrets relating to the opposite sex at all—although I wouldn't have minded sharing a few with Sergio! Stefania and I would indulge in repeat viewings of *Three Coins in the Fountain* at the Cremorne Orpheum Theatre and sigh in unison, dreaming of Italy.

My husband Bill and I have since been to Italy a total of nine times. With every visit, we become more passionate about its food, wine and people.

When I began relearning the language (fourteen was a long time ago!) I soon knew I had to write a book that truly captured the essence of Italy: the vitality of the gregarious, garrulous people; the robust, flavoursome food; the joyous music, the sheer happiness of being alive in one of Europe's most beautiful countries.

Everything in Italy is generous, the people, the spirit, the food—from the Austrian influence of the north to the African of the south. The language itself is boisterous yet seductive. I couldn't think of a better place to take seven enthusiastic writing students, all keen to write from dawn till dusk, inspired by the beautiful vista of vineyards in a Tuscan autumn.

Bill and I decided to write a book that would be as vibrant as Italy itself, about the fun we have had travelling there over the years—the people we've met, the food we've eaten, the joys of discovering the language, and the history of some of the most remarkable places we've seen.

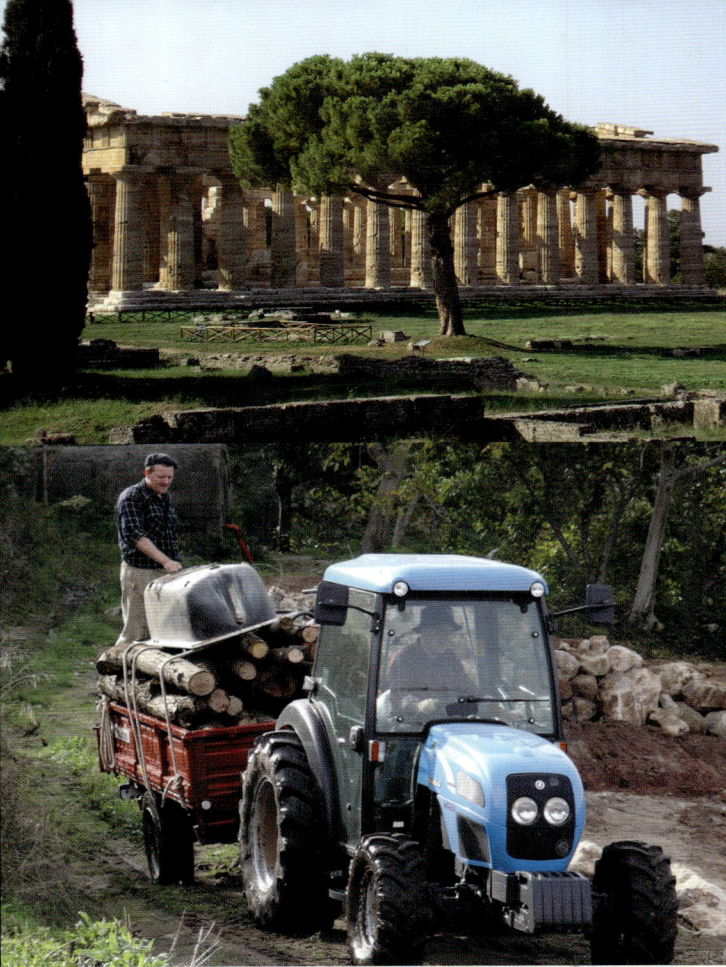

Past & Present

Before World War II, Italy was poor in comparison to the rest of Western Europe and unemployment forced many young men to migrate to find work. The war wrought huge destruction and great loss of life, but it was also a catalyst for change. The country made almost miraculous economic progress and, despite government instability, over the last decade Italy's per capita income was slightly ahead of Britain's and not much behind Germany and France. Yet there is a wonderful ambiguity to Italy—it is a land of contrasts. The prosperity and modernisation of the industrialised north (think Milan, Florence and Venice—or Armani, Alessi, Fiat and Ferragamo) gives way to the economically underdeveloped, largely agrarian south, which still attracts hordes of tourists each year, contrasting as it does with the northern snow-capped alps of the Dolomites and the glitzy Italian Riviera.

Even in industry there is a dichotomy between sophistication and simplicity: revenue is not only sourced from major industries such as car production, much of it is derived from family-owned-and-run companies that create beautiful handmade goods and gourmet foods.

Distinct variations in Italy's geographic regions resulted in a diversity of peoples, with northern Italians tending to be closer, geographically and temperamentally, to Germany and France, while southerners reflect invasions from North Africa and the eastern Mediterranean and the Bourbons from Spain. There is no such thing as a 'typical Italian' as there are so many local dialects, cuisines and customs.

Italy has more than 100 000 statues, churches, archaeological sites and cathedrals and Italians are very proud of their illustrious history. Modern architects, conscious of designing the new to complement the old, work within these confines and the balance between ancient and modern has been achieved remarkably well. It's not uncommon to find an elegant old church or a stunning cathedral just around the corner from a fast food outlet or an internet café.

Customs & culture

This vibrant, loud, fun-loving, macho, sassy, largely Catholic nation is a melting pot of people and cultural influences from Europe, Asia and Northern Africa. Having said that, three of its central cultural tenets have to be family, fun and fashion!

When it comes to haute couture, Italian designers are the undisputed kings of style. While elderly women wear long black dresses and headscarves, in the cities and in many small towns and villages, young women and men dress in style and parade each evening in the *passegiata* before dinner. From Armani to Moschino, Italian men are among the most elegant in Europe. They seem to have the knack of looking utterly chic in their chinos and loafers. Younger women often favour well-cut designer jeans teamed with tailored jackets. Shopping in any of the trendy stores is done against a background of techno music, replaced by Pavarotti in the upmarket boutiques.

Family life too is changing, and modern Italian women now often defy their traditional Catholic teachings to choose contraception. This is a country where practising Catholics grow fewer every year but still number about a billion worldwide. These same young women are still usually conservative enough to opt for a traditional white wedding.

Italian families are often large and children are indulged—the Italian appreciation of food, wine and love of life is fostered early. Friends and family members are typically effusive and ebullient. On greeting and parting, a kiss on each cheek is customary, with two kisses for those you know well and three kisses being popular if you know someone very well!

Language

Unless you know someone very well—or you're planning to—avoid telling them that you're *eccitata*. I say this because at the end of an exciting day's sightseeing in Rome I was practising my Italian on the helpful young men at the hotel reception, telling them, *sono molto eccitata*, which caused much amusement until I discovered the phrase also has the connotation of being sexually excited. Not the sort of confession one usually shares with the hotel staff!

The innate formality of Italians is apparent in their language, where degrees of familiarity exist. The formal *lei* (you) is used for those who are more senior or for someone whom you don't know, while the *tu* form is for greeting friends or peers. The nuances of language are always hard to acquire, but for most people conquering the mysterious rules of gender for words remains frustratingly out of reach. It really bothered Bill that beer was feminine, *la birra*, but wine, *il vino*, was masculine!

'There's simply no reason, darling,' I kept telling him, 'it's just the way it is.' He'd mumble under his breath but I had to agree it made learning Italian challenging, especially when some adjectives had to match the gender of nouns, but others didn't, and sometimes the article 'the' had to change to match the adjective ... and so it went on. One night Bill was struggling with, not only the buttons, but the gender of his shirt.

'How on earth can you talk about a man's shirt, *la camicia*, being feminine?' he complained.

I pointed out that Italians learning English had to cope with words like 'bough', 'cough' and 'rough', with very different pronunciations. He didn't say much after that (but he still mumbled!).

I don't know if the ancient Romans had as much trouble with gender in Latin, but if so it seems that the Latin alphabet spread beyond the borders of the Empire regardless—becoming the alphabet of western civilization.

Buongiorno: Good day

Come sta?: How are you?

Bene grazie: Good thank you

Mi chiamo…: My name is...

Come si chiama?: What is your name?

Potrebbe dirmi…?: Could you tell me...?

Sono di…: I'm from....

Per favore: Please

Si: Yes

No: No

Dov'è: Where is...?

Scusi: Excuse me

Prego: You're welcome

Arrivederci: Goodbye

Roman Holiday

I can't remember what excited me most on my first visit to Rome: the wonderful aura of ancient Rome that permeated architectural masterpieces such as the Trevi Fountain; waking up to the chime of church bells and the aroma of freshly brewed coffee to throw open the window to a kaleidoscope of colour bursting from the streets below; or—as is most likely for a single twenty-year-old, as I was then—waiting for a Rossano Brazzi lookalike to pinch my bottom. It never happened—and it never has!

Unfortunately, on this visit Bill and I arrived in pouring rain on the busiest night of the week at Rome airport—the only night that the shuttle bus to our hotel didn't operate (what a pity our travel agent hadn't thought to mention this in passing!). We couldn't find a taxi willing to take us the mere three kilometres to our airport hotel. They would pull up, wind down the window, then, when they heard where I wanted to go, yell '*Solo Roma!*' and leave us standing in the rain. I couldn't believe every taxi was 'only for Rome' but after twenty minutes I stormed into the chaos that is Rome airport and told three young policemen that all of the taxis were refusing to take me. One young *poliziotto* produced a whistle and delivered a blast that would have brought Caesar back from his grave and consequently three taxis screeched to a halt in front of me. One policeman helped us put our bags in the car; another held open the door for me. I felt like a celebrity! Within minutes we were on our way ... and FAST! Street signs, a blur of Italian directions, whizzed by, all merging into a background of sepia-toned buildings and honking, speeding traffic.

Italians are renowned for their reliance on the horn, and our taxi driver Gino was no exception. Despite the downpour, he drove erratically, turning around to make eye contact as he told us he was quitting taxi driving to work as a hair colourist. No wonder he was so interested in whether blonde was my natural colour!

When in Italy

It didn't take us long to adjust to the pace, sights and smells of life in Italy. Fashionably dressed young women clattered in their stilettos along the narrow, cobbled streets. Plump mammas carefully pored over every tomato before popping them into their string bags. Old men playing cards or *bocce* sat in the park, watching uninhibited young lovers embrace nearby. Darkly handsome young men, with cardigans draped casually over their shoulders, drank Campari in crowded sidewalk cafés. Boisterous children kicked a ball around the thousand-year-old statue in the piazza while their mothers sipped *cappuccini* and looked on.

Rome is one of the most sophisticated cities in the world and yet, in the honeycomb of narrow twisting streets opening to spacious squares, much of life goes on as it has done for centuries.

I really felt we could have pulled up a chair and stayed there for the rest of the day, but the Colosseum beckoned, as did the street artist I had glimpsed further ahead. I greeted him with '*Buongiorno*' and he beamed with delight. I was anxious to practise my Italian. Whenever I spoke it, I was amazed by the genuine pleasure it invoked. I was invariably asked if my mamma or papa were Italian, or perhaps my *nonna*? When I told people I learned the language because I love it and Italy, I made a new friend for life!

A simple enquiry of the artist about the price of a watercolour led to a ten-minute conversation about his cousin, who had migrated to America, which led to another ten-minute conversation about whether or not he, Georgio, would also be more successful if he were to migrate to America. We felt we couldn't leave him without buying something, so we chose a streetscene that captured the simple pleasures of Italian life.

Walking around the ancient city, we felt time seemed to have gone into neutral. We watched old women crocheting as they sat on their doorsteps and gossiped, or swept the cobblestones, pausing frequently to chat to passers-by.

We stopped to ask for directions. Some of the women wore the headscarves and mourning black of widows and occasionally wept softly into large lace handkerchiefs. Perhaps the fact that Italian custom demands that widows visit the cemetery every day to tend the grave of their dearly departed was the cause of their weeping. I'd be weeping too if I had to keep that up—especially if you were actually relieved that the old boy had finally passed on! In many houses and cafés, we could smell the aroma fresh garlic and basil, as bruschetta was being made. We decided to take a city tour and our erudite guide brought the crumbling stone

Bruschetta
with tomato and basil

Serves 4–6

1 ciabatta loaf or French baguette, cut into
  2 cm (¾ in) slices
olive oil, for brushing
2 garlic cloves, roasted and crushed
440 g (14 oz) Roma tomatoes, diced
1 small red (Spanish) onion, finely chopped
1 tablespoon fresh basil, chopped
1 tablespoon balsamic vinegar
2 tablespoons olive oil
salt and freshly ground black pepper, to taste

Grill bread slices for 2–3 minutes on each side. Brush each slice with a little olive oil and spread a thin layer of roasted garlic on each slice.

In a bowl, mix together tomato, onion, basil, vinegar and olive oil and season with salt and pepper.

Serve grilled bread with tomato mixture on top.

walls to life with stories of Rome's early history and its enemies: the Volscians, the Aequians, the Sabines and the Etruscans. I loved her story of the celebrated hero Cincinnatus. When the Aequians trapped both a Roman consul and his entire army, Cincinnatus was appointed dictator. He was ploughing when he heard the news, but immediately left his plough, assembled an army, defeated the enemy and then resigned, triumphant, to his farm—all in sixteen days!

I was overwhelmed by the absolute grandeur of Rome, not just the frescoes, friezes and sculptures, but by Rome's past as a powerful empire. At the height of its power, the Roman Empire comprised some 25 modern countries and boasted a population of over 50 million people.

Rome soon became the centre of the Christian world. In the Renaissance and Baroque periods, talented artists, architects and artisans were lured to create great works for popes and noble families, and it was during this period that many of the city's magnificent architectural masterpieces were created.

We strolled through the twisting back streets, interrupted only by the buzz of Vespas, their riders threading in and out of the throngs of pedestrians. By midmorning we paused for *gelati*, then carried on gazing at works of art of almost every architectural age. There was so much to distract us that we didn't make it to the Colosseum that day, but we did make it to a great little bar for an aperitif—or two! After three it seemed a good idea to eat. Our waiter at Al Picchio wasn't in the least surprised when Bill ordered Chicken Marsala and I ordered my favourite, Saltimbocca alla Romana.

Saltimbocca
alla Romana

Serves 4

400 g (14 oz) veal cut into 8 thin slices
120 g (4 oz) ham or prosciutto, cut into thin slices
16 sage leaves
45 g (1½ oz) unsalted butter
salt and freshly ground black pepper
2 tablespoons of dry white wine

Slice fat from the veal slices and half them. Cut the ham/prosciutto into small slices. Wash sage leaves and pat dry with kitchen towel. Spread out the veal slices and pound with a meat tenderiser. Lay a slice of ham and a sage leaf on the top, then roll them up and hold it all together with a toothpick.

Melt the butter in a flameproof casserole dish and arrange the Saltimbocca in the dish, season to taste and then cook them for 1–2 minutes. Once veal is browned, roll over and cook quickly on all sides. Remove Saltimbocca and pour the wine into the casserole dish, simmer for a few minutes, then serve it over the Saltimbocca as a sauce.

Around Rome

You can't see much of Rome without doing a lot of walking, but to relieve tired legs, buy a train ticket from the *cassa biglietti* (ticket office) or from the *tabaccàio*. If you get lost at the airport look for officials wearing ADR, (*Aeroporto di Roma*), elsewhere the *poliziotti* (policemen) are very helpful (and handsome!). A romantic way to travel is by *carrozza* (horse and carriage).

Things to see

- Stroll Capitoline Hill, once the centre of the Roman world where the city of Rome's three major temples were located.
- Imagine the roar of the crowds at the Colosseum (pictured here).
- Visit the Roman Forum, once the hub of politics in ancient Rome.
- Wander among the ruins on the Palatine Hill, which was the abode of Roman emperors and affluent aristocrats.
- Make a wish as you throw a coin into the Trevi Fountain.

Il giorno dopo

The aroma of coffee and the chime of church bells woke us early the next day (*il giorno dopo*). We dressed quickly and hurried downstairs to sip espresso from tiny cups in the next door *trattoria*. We drank our coffee at the bar, hoping to pass for locals; the real locals munched sweet bread rolls and read *Il Giornale*. Afterwards, we dawdled back to the hotel for breakfast, pausing to admire mouth-watering displays of dainty cakes, fresh fruits, salami and cheese, and exploring the winding narrow streets. Around us, Rome was bursting into life.

Our companion at breakfast was a gaunt young Australian man, a poet who was to spend most of the trip penning mournful love poems to his girlfriend. She'd made off with his best mate three days before they were to leave for the tour, so he'd brought his mum, Mavis, instead. Mavis had never been to Europe before and couldn't see any real need to visit this time either, except that Darren had paid for her and she couldn't really afford to waste his money. She told us she was sorry to be missing both her bingo and lawn bowls day—obviously both were very close to her heart. Mavis found it difficult to come to terms with the number of foreigners in Italy, 'I've never seen so many Italians!' and even harder to accept the concept of tipping. 'That waiter didn't do anything special. Just brought me Fanta like I asked for. And did you see the price of it? Twice what I pay back home! What'm I supposed to tip him for? Ripping me off?' Most of the meal she spent knitting, and calculating the enormous profit the Italians were making on Fanta sales.

At midday, we finally reached the Colosseum, the most famous of the Roman amphitheatres; underneath it runs a network of passages through which gladiators and animals made their grim journey to the arena. The ancient Romans were obsessed with 'sport', and the Colosseum could hold between 50 000 and 70 000 people. The Circus Maximus, one of several chariot racing tracks, could hold 250 000 spectators.

Much of the entertainment involved blood sports, with wild animal hunts and fights to the death for gladiators. In fact, the AD 108 games celebrating the conquest of Dacia (Romania) lasted for 123 days and involved the slaughter of 11 000 animals, as well as combat between some 10 000 gladiators. I don't know how people got so much time off work!

While we ate lunch, followed by a delicious dessert of Tiramisu, I thought that if I'd lived in ancient Rome I would have liked to visited the Baths of Caracalla, where people exercised, plunged into invigorating cold baths, or relaxed and chatted in the unisex steam rooms—where, it seems, Romans often 'picked up' a partner! A daily visit to the baths was an important part of Roman social life, a bit like today's gyms. Rome's wealthy citizens often spent all day there, taking their slaves with them to attend to habits such as rubbing oil (instead of soap) into the skin before scraping off the dirt and sweat with a razor-like implement called a *strigil*!

Tiramisu

Serves 4

250 g (8 oz) mascarpone
½ cup (4 fl oz) thickened (double) cream
2 tablespoons brandy
¼ cup (2 oz) sugar

2 tablespoons instant coffee powder
1½ cups (12 fl oz) boiling water
1 x 250 g (8 oz) packet sponge fingers
250 g (8 oz) chocolate, grated

Place mascarpone, cream, brandy and sugar in a bowl, mix to combine and set aside. Dissolve coffee powder in boiling water and set aside.

Line the base of a 20 cm (8 in) square dish with one-third of the sponge fingers. Sprinkle one-third of the coffee mixture over sponge fingers, then top with one-third of the mascarpone mixture. Repeat layers finishing with a layer of mascarpone mixture, sprinkle with grated chocolate and chill for 15 minutes before serving.

Note: If mascarpone is unavailable, mix one part sour cream with three parts lightly whipped thickened (double) cream and use in its place.

Religious Rome

Vatican city, on Vatican Hill in the north-western part of Rome, is the smallest independent land-locked nation in the world (if the Knights of Malta is disregarded) and covers an area of less than one square kilometre. The Pope is the Head of Government in this non-hereditary elective monarchy and wields absolute authority. He is elected for a life term and, with a billion Catholics in his fold, is one of the most powerful men in the world.

Some 900 people, mostly male, live inside the Vatican's walls—priests, nuns, dignitaries, and the famous Swiss Guard (a volunteer military force responsible for the Pope's security) resplendent in their red, yellow and blue uniforms.

The official language is Latin and whenever I see two priests talking I can't resist eavesdropping to see if they're actually speaking it. There is even Vatican City citizenship, which enables Vatican officials to travel on special passports, giving them diplomatic status in many countries. Vatican City has its own train station, Vatican Bank, postal service, radio station, telephone system, currency and even its own news-paper, *L'Osservatore Romano*. The city is tremendously wealthy. The grandeur of the architecture, paintings, sculpture, frescoes, tapestries, gold is overwhelming. I always feel the need to sit down to absorb it all. In St Peter's Square the immensity of the twelve apostles, gazing down at the hordes of tourists below, makes me wonder how the builders managed to position them. It would be an amazing feat today, but remembering the limitations the sculptors must have faced, it becomes even more incredible.

These days, security is tight. We had to line up and have our bags searched by x-ray before going into St Peter's basilica, which can hold up to 60 000 people. I never know where to look because there's so much to see and I don't want to miss anything.

The Basilica is crowded with international visitors and the atmosphere is hushed as people are awed by the splendid interior and its priceless treasures. The bronze statue of St Peter is magnificent, his right foot worn down from the stroking and kissing of millions of pilgrims over the years. Some initiates were actu-ally weeping! Every gallery boasts masterpieces by da Vinci, Raphael, Giotto, Caravaggio and Bellini. In the Sistine Chapel, my favourite, Michelangelo's frescoes alone are worth the visit. I don't know how he painted them on the ceiling—especially as I read somewhere that it took him over 15 years— just being up that high must have been nerve-racking! Surely nowhere else in the world can claim so much rich beauty and history in so small an area.

Coffee & cards

Everywhere in Italy, men sit drinking coffee, arguing politics and playing cards. The history of coffee involves political intrigue, the pursuit of wealth and power, papal intervention, and above all 'chance', for it was discovered entirely by accident!

The story goes that a goat herder noticed his goats were pretty frisky after eating some red berries. Curious, he nibbled a few and found he felt pretty frisky too! A passing monk chastised him for partaking of the devil's fruit but soon the monks discovered this fruit could help them stay awake for their prayers.

The coffee plant spread from Ethiopia and arrived in Venice around 1570. Only rich Venetians could afford coffee and it was sold only in chemists' shops! By 1640, the first coffee shop opened in Venice, soon to be followed by others, the most notable of which today are the Café Florian in Piazza San Marco in Venice, Caffe Greco in Rome, Pedrocchio in Padua, Michelangelo in Florence and Baratti in Turin. By 1763 there were 218 coffee shops in Venice alone.

The path to acceptance had not been easy. Some Christians claimed coffee was the favourite drink of the devil and asked Pope Clemente VII to ban Christians from drinking it. The Pontiff requested a sample to taste and allegedly declared, 'This beverage is so delicious it would be a sin to let only misbelievers drink it! Let's defeat Satan by blessing this beverage'—and bless it he did.

Once coffee had the Pope's seal of approval it was served in elegant coffee shops where patrons would sit for hours gossiping and eyeing one another off. Men of culture in the eighteenth century enjoyed coffee so much that it was described as an 'intellectual beverage' and was believed to have healing powers. Today, the word espresso has become almost synonymous with Italian coffee and there are more than 200 000 espresso bars all over Italy serving it, often in dainty, napkin-wrapped glasses on saucers.

Coff up!

In 1453, Turkish law made it legal for a woman to divorce her husband if he failed to provide her with her daily quota of coffee. I warned Bill that this law may be introduced in the Rowe household at any time!

Achilles Gaggia perfected the espresso machine, inventing cappuccino, so named because it resembles the colour of the robes worn by the monks of the Capuchin order.

Espresso cake

Serves 6–8

1 cup (8 fl oz) boiling water
¼ cup (2 oz) ground espresso coffee beans
200 g (6½ oz) melted butter
1¼ cup (10 oz) sugar
3 eggs, lightly beaten
1 tablespoon vanilla essence
2 cups (8 oz) plain (all-purpose) flour
3 teaspoons baking powder
8 sugar cubes
cinnamon

Coffee flavoured cream

1¼ cup (10 fl oz) fresh cream
1 tablespoon icing (confectioners') sugar
2 tablespoons of very strong espresso coffee chilled

Preheat oven to 180°C (350°F/Gas Mark 4).
Pour boiling water over first measure of coffee beans and leave to steep for 5 minutes. Strain liquid and pour over butter in a large bowl, stirring until butter melts. Mix in sugar, eggs and vanilla and beat with a wooden spoon until combined.

Sift flour and baking powder into mixture and mix in with second measure of coffee. Pour mixture into a 20 cm (8 in) springform cake tin lined with baking paper.

Bake for 50–55 minutes or until cake springs back when lightly touched. Crush sugar cubes and sprinkle over hot cake. Cool in tin for 10 minutes before turning onto a wire rack.

To make the Coffee Flavoured Cream, whip cream until soft. Beat in icing sugar and coffee. Dust cake with cinnamon and serve with Coffee Flavoured Cream.

vorrei—I'd like… *un espresso*—espresso (small shot of strong coffee) *la torta*— cake *il caffè*—coffee *lo zucchero*—sugar *la tazza*—cup *il latte*—milk *il tè*—tea *macchiato*—espresso with a drop of milk *cappucino freddo*—iced coffee *affogato*— espresso with a spoon of ice cream

Getting around

Our rental car was delivered to us mid-morning and, with the sky grey and bleak and the rain still drizzling, we left Rome and set off for Castel del Piano, near the city of Grosseto.

Bill and I have a system for getting around any country—I drive and he navigates—a system that has had its successes and failures over the years. Getting out of Rome was one of the failures! I knew it was a failure when we turned a corner in the road and I saw waves breaking over rocks on my right. According to the map, had we been going the correct way, north, the water would be on my left. An easy enough mistake to make, heading south rather than north, but it was not helped by the madcap motorbike drivers, the honking horns and the Italian road signs.

We attempted to change course on one of Rome's many large roundabouts. After three unsuccessful attempts to exit, I put my fist on the horn like every other Italian driver circling me, and held it there! I changed down to third gear and yelled at Bill to put his arm out the window to indicate I was about to cut across the traffic to the exit. It worked! We were on the exit, finally heading north.

As you might have gathered, getting around Italy is certainly no easy task. We often saw confusing road signs facing in different directions but bearing the same city on the sign!

Throughout our trip I tried various methods of transport, from the popular motorbike, to swiftly gliding gondolas in the canals of Venice. We also saw many charming little cars perfect for zipping down the busy streets. But by far the most amazing vehicle I came across on my travels was the car (bottom left), whose rural owner rather proudly told me that they didn't use the car much, only when they went into town, but that it went well once they cleared out all the hay! I was thankful that our small Mercedes hire car was in better condition.

Some hours (and more than a few wrong turns) later, we lurched down the very narrow, unmade road to the farm where we were to stay with our friends Alvina and Umberto.

I had bought some biscotti and grissini from a *pasticceria* to nibble on when we stopped for our usual picnic morning tea. The drive was very pretty. The mountains were surrounded by woods and the road was fringed with tall trees and littered with spiky chestnut husks. We often glimpsed a lone figure gathering chestnuts or wild porcini mushrooms in the roadside forests.

Biscotti

Makes about 40

70 g (2 oz) blanched almonds
2 cups (9 oz) plain (all-purpose) flour
1 teaspoon baking powder
pinch of salt
½ cup (4 oz) caster sugar
1 teaspoon vanilla essence
2 eggs
½ cup shelled pistachio nuts
1 egg white

Preheat oven to 180°C (350°F/Gas Mark 4).
Toast almonds for 5–10 minutes or until pale golden brown.
Allow to cool, then chop roughly. Sift flour, baking powder
and salt into a bowl. Add caster sugar and combine. Lightly
beat vanilla essence and eggs, then add to dry ingredients. Mix until well combined. Turn onto a lightly floured
surface and work in the nuts. Add more flour if necessary
until a firm dough is reached.

Divide in half and shape into logs about 5 cm (2½ in)
wide. Place on greased baking tray. Lightly beat egg white
then brush each log. Bake for 35 minutes or until cooked
through. Once cool, cut each log diagonally into 1 cm (½
in) slices. Reduce oven to 150°C (300°F Gas Mark 2).
Bake for 10 minutes on a baking tray or until dry.

Grissini

Makes 20 sticks

1 tablespoon malt (or golden) syrup
2 tablespoons olive oil
1¼ cups (10 fl oz) warm water
500 g (1 lb) unbleached bread flour
1 tablespoon yeast
2 tablespoons salt
½ cup (4 oz) sesame or poppy seeds

Preheat oven to 220°C (425°F/Gas Mark 7).
Combine malt syrup, oil and warm water. Add to flour
together with yeast and salt. Mix until well combined. Turn
out onto a floured surface and knead until smooth and
elastic. Shape dough into a ball, brush surface with oil and
allow to rise for an hour. When ready to shape, deflate
dough and flatten. Cut dough into four pieces then cut
each piece into strips about 1 cm (1⅓ in) thick. Shape by
holding each end of the strip and pulling gently until the
strip is about 20 cm (8 in) long or by dividing dough into
20 small pieces and rolling each of these out to form long
sticks about 30 cm (12 in) long.

Spray sticks with water and then roll in sesame seeds
or poppy seeds. Place sticks on a baking tray. There is no
need to let the grissini rise. Spray with water and bake for
20 minutes until crisp and golden.

Prego!

Our friends Alvina and Umberto have been married for three years and although they came to Tuscany to buy a little place to live in for a couple of months a year, they have fallen in love with the area and now spend ten months of the year there, returning to Australia only for November and December.

The farm is bounded by the village of Castel del Piano at the top, a creek at the bottom of the vineyard, the Montegiovi road which leads to the village, and the *antica strada* (an old donkey and walking track) just below the main farmhouse.

Our friends welcomed us effusively answering our thanks for their hospitality with 'Prego', which means both 'you're welcome' and 'please'.

When Alvina and Umberto bought the property it was completely overgrown with ivy and blackberries and foxes had made their home in the lower floors of the three very dilapidated houses on the site, which had also been given over to the cows and pigs.

Bill and I had been perplexed by the ramshackle ruins we'd seen on previous visits to Italy and could never understand why anyone would keep them standing, but Umberto explained that the law prevents new houses being built, so people buy these ruins and 'restore' them even though it is often like rebuilding from the floor up! The smell of the livestock took weeks to get rid of and Alvina is sure her back won't recover from weeks of stripping back the original chestnut doors. But restoration is now complete.

Castel del Piano is away from the popular tourist track. It's a medieval village set in a picturesque Tuscan valley fringed with olive groves and vineyards.

Narrow alleys in the town weave through tiny squares and even tinier stairways lead to shops selling delicious fresh pasta, homemade gelato and cakes. Each September, Castel del Piano plays host to the Palio delle Contrade, a three-day horse racing event that dates back to the fifteenth century.

Just a short drive away from the village is the Romanesque abbey church of Sant'Antimo where the monks sing mass in Latin Gregorian chant at 11 o'clock each day. Close by is Montalcino, a pretty hilltop village and home to the famous Brunello red wine.

Every village in Italy has a tale to tell. Montalcino's is that the citizens of Siena fled to the town to defend themselves from the imperial army, until they were suppressed in 1559. Also nearby is the spa town of Bagno Vignone and the gardens of La Foce, where Anglo-American writer the Marchese Iris Origo wrote her *Diary of the War in the Val d'Orcit*.

On the farm

Alvina's eight-hectare farm is about one and a half kilometres along a narrow country road bordered either side by a 100-year-old chestnut (*castagna*) forest, hazelnuts (*nocciola*) and walnut (*noce*) trees, as well as fruit trees—cherries, apples, quinces, apricots, figs, pears, persimmons and almonds. Castel del Piano and Seggiano are both hilltop villages, nearly 70 kilometres from Siena, 650 metres above sea level and housing around 4000 people.

Alvina and Umberto are restoring three cottages and plan to enjoy an *agriturismo* lifestyle. They live in the main house, called Podernuovo. Bill and I stayed in Il Seccatoio, which was originally a chestnut drying house and was later used as a pen for birds and rabbits. The chestnuts were brought in up a ramp at the back of the top floor and laid out on large timber boards. On the ground floor a slow fire burned for at least forty days to dry the chestnuts. They were then ground into a flour called *pulendo*, a staple for the local population for many years.

The building has been rebuilt and restored using the original stone, chestnut beams and handmade roof tiles. When renovating, Umberto found a family of tortoises ensconced behind the dry stone walls of the house! Wild boar and deer also lived on the farm.

Outside the house is a flourishing vegetable garden and a newly planted vineyard and olive grove. Two springs provide fresh water.

Il Seccatoio was beautiful—quaint and rustic with a huge terrace overlooking the vinyard, but with excellent plumbing. It also had a modern kitchen that I soon christened, eager to begin my initiation into Tuscan cooking.

History

The Tuscan provinces of Florence, Arezzo, Grosetto, Livorno, Pisa and Siena are the birthplace of the Renaissance, but also contain around 120 nature reserves.

Rustic romance

Just before sunset each day, Bill and I would walk through the narrow, tree-lined lanes around Podernuovo, which were bordered with wildflowers and berries. We'd delight in clambering over fences to explore crumbling stone cottages where nesting doves cooed from the rooftops. Sometimes we came across old carts or rusty wagons, their wheel spokes covered in creepers, or a half-buried plough, once much-used by a farmer long since dead, his children perhaps grown up and gone to the city.

Quail with lemon & sage

Serves 4

4 tablespoons olive oil
1 tablespoon lemon juice
½ teaspoon lemon rind
1 clove of garlic, crushed
freshly ground black pepper to taste
sea salt

2 tablespoons olive oil,
4 quails, butterflied
1 bunch sage leaves (1 tablespoon chopped and the rest for garnish)
¼ cup (2 fl oz) chicken stock

Preheat oven to 180°C (350°F/Gas Mark 4).
Combine olive oil, lemon juice, lemon rind, garlic, pepper and salt in a bowl and set aside. Heat 1 tablespoon of the extra oil in a large pan, then add quail and chopped sage leaves and brown quickly. Set aside in a baking dish. Add the remaining oil, lemon juice mixture and chicken stock. Return to heat, bring to the boil, and simmer for 1 minute (to reduce liquid), stirring with a wooden spoon.
Pour pan juices over quail and bake in the oven for 20–25 minutes. Garnish with whole sage leaves.

Lunch & locals

Lunch in Italy is still regarded by many as the main meal of the day. It is usually a leisurely meal, followed by a siesta. We often enjoyed ours on the huge stone terrace that overlooked a valley dotted with stone cottages. Monte Amiata loomed blue in the distance.

A few days into our stay, Alvina invited some of the local expats to join us—Lolette Oliphant, a charming 88-year-old woman who lived in Naples for four years until her Italian husband died; and Rosemary and Hilary Jenkins, a delightful couple who have lived in Tuscany for years. Lolette was one of the most fascinating women I've met in a long time. She's writing a book about her life and I'm sure it will be an enthralling read, having had four husbands—two Greek and two Italian. Hilary was a historian at the University of Dublin, and Rosemary was a history teacher. Both knew a lot about the history of the area.

Alvina served a delicious fennel and orange salad and walnut and pesto pasta followed by poached figs and homemade ice cream for dessert. It was so delicious that I managed to polish it off despite feeling as though I couldn't eat another mouthful—a regular feeling for me in Italy!

The pace of each day is slower in Italy. The ritual of lunch followed by a siesta segments the day into morning and evening. This form of mid-afternoon relaxation is still observed in country villages and even in the city many people still return home for a hearty lunch of soup, pasta or a main course and take a nap before returning to work. After lunch I felt no hesitation in climbing into bed at three o'clock … as they say, *Quando a Roma, fai come fanno i Romani* … When in Rome, do as the Romans do… I'm sure that saying must apply equally to Tuscany!

Fennel and orange salad

Serves 6

1 bunch curly endive (frisée), leaves separated and washed
1 small fennel bulb, cut into thin strips
3 oranges, peeled and segmented
1 onion, sliced
20 black olives

Orange dressing
3½ tablespoons olive oil
3 tablespoons white wine vinegar
1 tablespoon fresh fennel leaves, chopped
½ teaspoon orange rind, grated
½ teaspoon sugar
freshly ground black pepper to taste

Place endive on a large serving platter. Arrange fennel, oranges, onion and olives attractively over endive.
To make the orange dressing, place oil, vinegar, fennel, orange rind, sugar and black pepper in a screw-top jar. Shake well to combine. Pour dressing over salad and serve immediately.

Alvina's walnut pesto pasta

Serves 4

400g (13 oz) cappellini pasta
sea salt and black pepper to taste
large bunch of fresh basil leaves
2 cloves of garlic
1 large handful of chopped walnuts
extra virgin olive oil
½ cup of grated parmesan cheese

Place pasta into boiling water with a little salt and cook for around 15 minutes or until *al dente,* which means firm to bite.

Shred basil leaves and place in a blender with peeled and crushed cloves of garlic, walnuts and about 3 tablespoons of olive oil. Puree until smooth and then add the parmesan cheese and a little more olive oil.

Add a few more finely chopped walnuts and parmesan to taste. Pour over the drained pasta and garnish with a sprig of fresh basil.

Back to nature

From wherever you are on the farm, the imposing profile of Monte Amiata, the highest mountain in Tuscany, can be seen in the distance. The entire region around the 1738-metre-high mountain is a haven for wildlife and flora. Numerous nature reserves protect roe deer, porcupines, badgers, foxes, squirrels, the Marsican bear and the threatened Apennine wolf, which was considered on the brink of extinction in the 1970s but is slowly increasing in number thanks to research programs in the Majella, Gran Sasso and Monti della Laga National Parks.

Winter is snowy in the mountains but during the warm summers dense forests of beech, pine, fir, oak, yew, maple and chestnut cover the hills, occasionally breaking onto grassy clearings that blaze with wildflowers, particularly poppies. Many species of birds and reptiles also make their home on Monte Amiata. Bill and I didn't get to see an Apennine wolf—not even from a safe distance—but we did meet one of the pricklier inhabitants of the area, a porcupine. Porcupines are now a protected species, and although they don't look very appetising to me, they had long been considered a food source and were eaten throughout the region!

I spent my mornings getting back to nature, sitting on the sunny pergola off the villa kitchen just a little way from Cosimo and Concetta, two rare Amiata donkeys who occupied their own donkey house next to our villa.

Once the main source of transport and farm power for the valley, Amiata donkeys are now protected by a special program to maintain the species, of which there are only around 200 left. Cosimo and Concetta are particularly fortunate because Alvina and Umberto had them microchipped and built a lovely warm donkey house for them, a fact that amused and astonished local farmers who think the *stranieri* (strangers) from Australia are very odd indeed. A house for the donkeys! What next?

Each afternoon we climbed up the hill behind our villa to help feed the donkeys, who skittered down the steep incline as soon as they spied the red bucket of apples, braying all the way. They are very affectionate; Concetta nuzzled right up again my chest and loved to have her nose stroked, while Cosimo pushed in for his share.

In this tranquil valley we were interrupted only by the hammering of the workmen putting the finishing touches to the third cottage. The daily feeding ritual bemused the workmen, who stopped chipping at the rocks to gaze in amazement at the fuss that four *stranieri* were making of two donkeys.

Buon appetito

Our first dinner was in front of the wood fire in Alvina's kitchen (that's Alvina bottom right). Umberto made an antipasto of sun-dried tomatoes, olives and fresh zucchini carpaccio marinated in lemon oil with parmigiano, followed by a delicious spinach and riscotta cannelloni and a salad of witlock and bitter leaves (Italians swear it aids digestion). We ate and drank and gossiped in true Italian style until late in the night.

Italians tend to buy only in-season fruit and vegetables, so a tomato salad with fresh-picked basil is a distinctly summer delicacy. Most Italians also make tomatoes into a tasty sauce that is bottled and stored in the pantry to use as a base for tomato dishes throughout the year. Vegetables bought during their season are preserved in oil for later use, while raw vegetables are often served with *bagna cauda* (a classic anchovy dipping sauce) or stuffed and cooked.

It's incorrect to think of Italian food as one distinct cuisine—even the eight regions of what is roughly defined as northern Italy have very different cooking styles, as varied as the dialects spoken.

Meat is more commonly eaten in the north, except for areas such as Liguria and the Adriatic coast, where seafood is more plentiful. Cheese, vegetables, mushrooms, grains, legumes and herbs, along with pasta, polenta and gnocchi, are always popular. Pasta is often served as a starter, followed by a meat dish and then dessert. Rice is used to make risotto and to bulk up broth and soups.

The northen regions also produce about a third of Italian wine and its by-product, the popular grappa.

Chilli peppers, spices, garlic and herbs are the essential ingredients of the more robust southern cooking, although in the south, like the north, cuisine varies throughout six regions and reflects the culinary legacy of the Greeks, Etruscans, Saracens, French, Spaniards and Arabs.

Olive oil is fundamental to all Italian cooking, but the symbol of southern Italian cuisine is the tomato (*pomodoro*), along with peppers (*pepperoni*), beans (*fagioli*), potatoes (*patate*) and eggplant (*melanzane*). Pasta was reportedly first served in the south.

In the south, meat is eaten inland and almost every scrap of beef, veal or lamb is stewed, braised, grilled, fried or roasted. Nothing is wasted and bones are used in recipes such as Osso buco. Poultry, hare, boar and game birds are often found on menus, as is pork.

Italians also enjoy puddings and ices, often flavoured with almond, nuts, honey, raisins and figs.

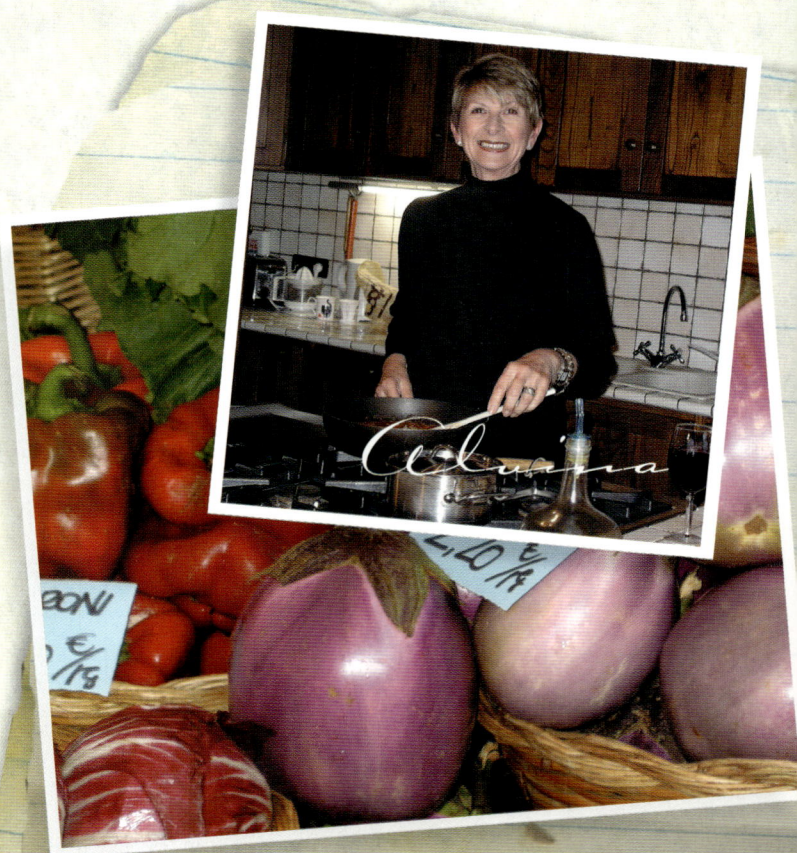

Spinach and ricotta cannelloni
with tomato sauce

Serves 4

2 tablespoons olive oil
½ cup shallots
410 g (13 oz) fresh ricotta
100 g (3 oz) prosciutto, chopped
½ bunch English spinach, blanched and chopped
2 tablespoons thickened (double) cream
pinch of nutmeg
salt and freshly ground black pepper to taste
16 cannelloni tubes

Tomato sauce
⅓ cup (2¾ fl oz) olive oil
2 cloves of garlic, crushed
2 medium onions, chopped
1 kg (2 lb) Roma tomatoes, peeled and seeded
2 teaspoon fresh oregano
2 teaspoon fresh rosemary, roughly chopped
2 tablespoons balsamic vinegar
2 tablespoons tomato paste
salt and freshly ground black pepper to taste
2 tablespoons romano cheese, grated

Preheat oven to 180°C (350°F/Gas Mark 4).

Heat oil in a pan and sauté shallots for 3–5 minutes until soft. In a bowl, mix together ricotta, prosciutto, spinach, shallots, cream, nutmeg, salt and pepper. Fill cannelloni tubes with mixture. Set aside.

To make tomato sauce, heat oil in a saucepan, add garlic and onion and cook for 5 minutes until soft. Add tomatoes, oregano, rosemary, balsamic vinegar, tomato paste and salt and pepper. Bring to the boil and leave to simmer with lid on for 30 minutes, or until it reaches a nice consistency.

In a baking dish, spoon in a layer of tomato sauce, then a layer of cannelloni. Repeat the layers, covering with tomato sauce, and sprinkling the top with cheese. Cover with foil and bake in oven for 30–40 minutes.

Osso buco

Serves 4

30 g (1 oz) butter
1 carrot, peeled and chopped
2 onions, chopped
2 sticks celery, chopped
2 cloves of garlic, crushed
4 thick slices of shin veal on the bone
plain (all-purpose) flour to coat
2 tablespoons olive oil
8 tomatoes, peeled and chopped
½ cup (4 fl oz) dry white wine
1 cup (8 fl oz) beef stock
1 bay leaf
freshly ground black pepper to taste
1 tablespoon butter mixed with 2 tablespoons plain (all-purpose) flour

Preheat oven to 180°C (350°F/Gas Mark 4).
Melt butter in a frying pan and cook carrot, onions, celery and garlic gently for 5 minutes or until vegetables are softened. Remove vegetables from pan and place in an ovenproof dish.
    Coat veal in flour. Heat oil in a frying pan and cook veal until golden on each side.
    Remove from pan and arrange over vegetables. Add tomatoes and cook, stirring constantly, for 5 minutes. Blend in wine, stock, bay leaf and finely grated black pepper, bring to the boil and simmer for 5 minutes. Whisk in butter mixture and pour over meat and vegetables. Cover dish and bake for 1½ hours or until meat is tender.

Gremolata
4 tablespoons fresh parsley, chopped
1 tablespoon lemon rind,
1 clove of garlic, crushed
1 anchovy, finely chopped

To make the gremolata, combine parsley, lemon rind, garlic and anchovy. Sprinkle gremolata over meat just prior to serving.

Fig puddings
with butterscotch sauce

250 g (8oz) chopped dried figs
1 cup (8 fl oz) water
1 teaspoon bicarbonate of soda
2 eggs
60 g (2 oz) butter
185 g (6 oz) caster sugar
185 g (6 oz) self-raising flour
1 teaspoon vanilla essence
1 vanilla bean

Butterscotch sauce
1 cup (5 oz) brown sugar
210 ml (7fl oz) fresh cream
30 g (1 oz) unsalted butter
fresh pouring cream to serve

Preheat oven to 190 ° C (375° F/Gas Mark 5.)
Place figs, water and bicarbonate of soda in a sauce-pan, and cook for about 20 minutes or until mixture reaches a jam-like consistency.

Pour fig mixture into a bowl, and beat in the remaining ingredients. Split vanilla bean down middle, scrape out the seeds and add them to the mixture.

Pour mixture into individual ramekins or muffin moulds and bake in the oven for 25 minutes.

To make the butterscotch sauce, combine all the ingredients in a saucepan and stir over a low heat until dissolved.

Serve individual puddings with butterscotch sauce and either pouring cream or ice cream.

Let's Start with Oil

The Mediterranean diet is one of the healthiest in the world, largely due to the ingredient that the Roman poet Homer called 'liquid gold'—olive oil. Rich in mono-unsaturates, antioxidants, vitamin E and plant compounds called polyphenols, olive oil has no salt, carbohydrate or sugar.

Olive oil cultivation is one of the oldest signs of civilisation, preceding writing. Now, there are over 800 million olive trees worldwide and over 400 varieties.

Roman mythology credits the first olive to Hercules, who struck the ground and caused an olive tree to sprout. Regarded as a symbol of peace, life and fertility, the trees were held in such esteem that only virgins and chaste men could tend the groves! Fortunately, growers today are not as stringent in their requirements!

Some historians claim olive oil is native to Iran, dating back over 5000 years. Others suggest Egypt, but with the expansion of the Roman Empire, olive oil soon spread to the Mediterranean. Fossilised remains of the olive tree's ancestor from 20 million years ago have been discovered near Livorno in Italy. When the Roman Empire declined, so did olive oil production, but by 1100 AD it regained importance and Tuscany became renowned for olive oil as groves flourished in the Tuscan climate. By 1400 AD, Italy had become the world's greatest producer of olive oil, and laws—still followed today—were passed to regulate its cultivation and sale.

According to Italian folklore, the perfect habitat for the olive tree is sun, stone, silence, solitude—and drought. They flourish in warm, dry summers and rainy winters and are so hardy they'll survive harsh

Villa Branca oil

The Chianti Classico Extra Virgin Olive Oil Villa Branca DOP is made by olives picked only by hand from the end of October to the end of November. The olives are crushed in the farm press, *frantoio*, a few hours after picking, using the traditional cold pressing method. The oil is then only lightly filtered before bottling.

Ancient oil sellers

In ancient times, one of the most flourishing trades was that of olive oil vendor. Oil was used for cooking, but also in lamps and as a soap substitute. Huge quantities were traded daily; so much so that there were 2300 oil sellers by 300 AD in Rome.

Seggiano oil

Seggiano Extra Virgin Olive Oil is made from an ancient olive variety called Olivastra Seggianese, unique to the town of Seggiano (far right) and surrounds on Monte Amiata. The oil is produced in the same way as in centuries past, with natural fertilisers and no pesticides. The olives are hand-picked with nets and ladders and stone-milled without delay. The resultant oil, bottled unfiltered, is sweet, delicate and creamy with just the right amount of pepperiness on the finish.

Basil oil

1½ (32 oz) fresh basil leaves
¼ (1 oz) pine nuts, toasted
2 cloves of garlic, chopped
25 g parmesan cheese, finely grated
25 g pecorino cheese, finely grated
⅓ cup (2 ¾ fl oz) olive oil
salt and freshly ground black pepper to taste

Place basil, pine nuts, garlic and cheese in a food processor and process until a paste forms. Add the oil to the running food processor and blend until it is all well combined. Season with salt and pepper. Pour the mixture into a jar and then pour a little extra olive oil on top to stop the basil from going brown. Store in the fridge.

Pinzimonio

Pinzimonio is an oil particularly popular for dipping vegetables.
½ cup of extra virgin olive oil
3 tablespoons lemon juice
½ teaspoon salt
fresh vegetables of your choice

Add the oil and lemon juice to a bowl and beat with a fork until well combined. Add the salt. Wash vegetables and cut them into the shape and size of your choice, although I'd recommend long strips.
Place oil in a small dipping bowl near the vegetable platter.

winters and scorching summers. Some trees live between 300–600 years and even when their branches or trunks die, these seemingly invincible trees often sprout again!

The consistency and colour of olive oil varies, much like fine wines due to varietal, climate and geographical differences. Afficionados distinguish three types—extra virgin, virgin and olive oil. Extra-virgin olive oil, which is less than 0.5 percent acidity and is produced by the first pressing of the olive, is considered the best oil with outstanding colour and flavour. It's best used cold for dipping bread or to drizzle over salads. Extra virgin olive oil has no proteins, it is a fat. A healthy fat! It contains antioxidant vitamin E and contains the highest percentage of mono-unsaturated fats in proportion to saturated and polyunsaturates.

Cooking with olive oil is similar to cooking with wine—the result will depend on the quality. Oil that is ordinary will produce ordinary results; the best oil produces the best dish.

Some years ago, Bill and I went to an olive oil tasting that was conducted with all the flourish and grandeur of a wine tasting. Until meeting Roberto, I had no idea anyone could be so passionate about olive oil. He stroked the vats lovingly as he told us that we were to judge on aroma, flavour and colour, which can range from a pale yellow to a greenish gold (although he added that at official DOC olive oil tastings the oil is served in opaque containers so the tasters can't be influenced by the colour).

'For flavour, you must be putting tongue and mouth to work. You must roll the oil through from the front tongue to the back tongue and then to the throat.'

Unfortunately, my roll went down the wrong way and I swallowed. Roberto was alarmed. 'No no, signora, not to swallow. No swallowing—only rolling,' he pleaded, his hands clasped prayer-like before him.

I rolled better the next time and Roberto relaxed.

'Can you taste her flowers? Her fruit?'

Not wanting to hurt his feelings, I nodded enthusiastically. 'Yes, the flowers, Roberto, I can taste the flowers.'

He beamed. 'Which flowers, signora?'

'All of them, Roberto. All of them' I answered as I wondered what fate would befall me for telling such wicked lies. I swirled the oil around to wet the sides of the tasting cup, to further release the oil's aroma while a buxom woman from Oklahoma swore black and blue she could taste fruit. Roberto was thrilled.

'Today this is a very good class. Yesterday's class was terrible people. No one could taste no thing.'

They might not have been able to taste anything, but I bet they all had a clear conscience afterwards!

Erbe

It's impossible for Italians to talk without using their hands, and it's impossible to cook Italian food without herbs (*erbe*)—preferably fresh ones. If they are dried, use one teaspoon for every tablespoon of fresh herbs required. Essential herbs for Italian cooking are oregano (*oregano*), sage (*salvia*), rosemary (*rosmarino*), basil (*basilico*), thyme (*time*) and parsley (*prezzemolo*).

Sage is used mostly in northern Italy and Tuscany and its silvery green leaves with their pebbled texture can be dipped in batter and fried for a delicious antipasto. The herb is thought to have originated in Syria, but in ancient Greek and Roman times it was used mostly as a healing herb (to relieve snake bites, eye problems, infection, epilepsy, intoxication, memory loss, worms—even as an aphrodisiac!)

Rosemary is used to flavour roasts, veal, pork and liver. Always chop its thick leaves as finely as possible and use them cautiously, as rosemary is strongly flavoured but mellows with cooking.

Basil or sweet basil, native to tropical Asia, is a tender low-growing herb with a pungent, sweet smell. It is used to season pizza, tomatoes, meats and sauces and is best added at the last minute, as cooking destroys its flavour. The herb can be preserved for a longer time in the freezer after blanching. Basil is sometimes used with fruit and in jams and sauces—especially with strawberries.

Thyme is a powerful herb that is best used sparingly to season meat, stuffings or marinades.

Spicy oregano is used in Mediterranean sauces, vegetable dishes and to flavour meat. It is commonly used on pizza.

Finally, flat Italian parsley adds flavour to almost any dish.

Torta d'erbe

Rita Pelliccia, who has lived in Pontremoli for some 26 years and owns Pizzeria Oscar, makes this delicious Torta, which is different from anything I have had before. Bill and I used to head down there every morning for our espresso and sit with the locals in her tiny pizzeria soaking up the atmosphere and eating her out of house and home.

1½ kg silver beet or spinach
¼ cabbage
2–3 onions
2–3 zucchini
1 leek
2 potatoes
½ kg ricotta
300 g parmesan, grated
2 tablespoons finely chopped parsley

Wash and dice the vegetables into small pieces, cover with a little salt and leave for half an hour. Drain off the excess liquid. Add ricotta and grated parmesan and chopped parsley and mix well.

For the pastry, use 2 cups plain white flour, a pinch of salt and 1 teaspoon of olive oil. Add a touch of water and mix. Use fresh pastry immediately.

Spread the vegetable mixture on top of the layer of pastry and then place another thin layer of the pastry on top. Prick and brush with oil and a little water. Pre-heat oven to 160°C (325°F, Gas Mark 3), bake in shallow rectangular tray for 40 minutes. Allow to cool before cutting into small squares to serve as an appetizer or larger squares to serve with a tossed salad as a luncheon dish.

Sage butter zucchini

Serves 4

6 zucchini (courgettes), trimmed and cut into 2 cm pieces
30 g (1 oz) butter
2 tablespoons fresh sage, chopped
salt and freshly ground black pepper to taste
2 tablespoons parmesan cheese, grated
2 tablespoons roasted pine nuts

Steam zucchini until just cooked. Place in a serving dish.
   Heat butter in a small saucepan, add sage and cook butter until brown. Season with salt and pepper.
Pour butter mixture over zucchini and then add grates parmesan cheese and pine nuts. Serve immediately.

Minestrone

Serves 4

60 g (2 oz) butter
2 cloves of garlic, crushed
2 small onions, finely chopped
4 rashers of bacon, rind removed, chopped
1 x 125 g (4 oz) can red kidney beans
100 g (3½ oz) green beans, trimmed
½ small cabbage, roughly chopped
3 medium-sized potatoes, peeled
   and chopped
2 carrots, peeled and diced

150 g (4½ oz) fresh or frozen peas, shelled
1 stick celery, chopped
2 tablespoons fresh parsley, finely chopped
2 l (64 fl oz) chicken stock
100 g (3½ oz) spinach, washed and chopped
50 g (2 oz) pasta of your choice
fresh parmesan cheese, shaved, to serve
salt to taste

In a deep pot, heat butter and add garlic, onion and bacon. Sauté for 4–5 minutes until onion is soft.
   Add all other ingredients to the pot (except spinach and pasta) and bring to the boil. Turn down heat and allow mixture to simmer, covered, for around 90 minutes. The vegetables should be tender.
Stir in spinach, then pasta, and cook pasta until *al dente* or firm to the bite (about 15 minutes).
   Serve with shaved parmesan cheese on top.

Antipasto

Antipasto—*anti* (before) and *pasto* (meal)—whets your appetite and gives you a taste for the delights that are to follow. Antipasto can be as substantial as you care to make it, or even a meal in itself, a supper after the theatre, or a superb brunch.

A few well-chosen bits and pieces can create an impressive spread when unexpected guests arrive, although I doubt that the antipasto we had of Seggiano olives, anchovy spread on celery stalks, prosciutto wrapped with fresh melon, shaved curls of parmigiano reggiano cheese and marinated artichokes and mushrooms, was thrown together too spontaneously!

Whenever we drop in to see friends in Italy we find that they are *sempre pronti*—ready to whip up an antipasto at a moment's notice.

Whether the food is to be part of a long lunch or something to graze on while enjoying a glass of wine will decide how lavish the antipasto should be. It also depends on which region you come from.

Usually, Italians provide two or three varieties of cured meats, perhaps a salami and a mortadella; hard-boiled eggs with mayonnaise; olives; fresh asparagus; pesto bruschetta; or some very fresh bocconcini and ripe tomatoes with a drizzle of oil and a little basil.

Italians seldom drink wine without eating and antipasto makes the perfect accompaniment.

60

Very vinegar

The fact that wine, beer or any liquid with less than 18 per cent alcohol becomes vinegar was an accidental discovery. Vinegar can be made from cane sugar, fruit juices, honey, molasses—even champagne!

Vinegar has been used for hundreds of years as a condiment, preservative, cleaning agent, beverage, wound remedy and antibiotic—Helen of Troy apparently bathed in it! Hippocrates, a Greek physician and writer, prescribed drinking vinegar to his patients for many ailments.

In the seventeenth century, vinegar was used as a deodorant and citizens held vinegar-soaked cloths to their noses to mask the stench of raw sewage in the city streets.

Ancient records mention Caesar's armies using vinegar as a beverage. According to the writings of Titus Livius, a historian who lived around the time of Christ, during road construction, obstructive boulders were heated and drenched in vinegar, cracking them into fragments that could be easily moved. The British Navy even used vinegar to clean the decks of their ships! I can only imagine what these vinegars must have tasted like!

An Italian friend, Anna la Torraca, told me that many older Italian women still make their vinegar in the traditional way, leaving wine or beer in a wooden cask for two to six months until it slowly turns to vinegar; some add a piece of pasta to speed up the process. It can then be filtered into another cask and left to mature for months, even years.

Red wine vinegar is left to age for longer than white wine vinegar. Balsamic vinegar has become very popular and the first reference to it is from the Italian town of Modena in 1046 AD.

Commercially, wine is poured over wood chips in giant vats and as it trickles down it takes on some of the flavour of the wood. Airborne bacteria uses oxygen in the air around the woodchips to oxidise the alcohol and turn it into acetic acid, but the subtle flavours of cask maturation are lost.

The best wine makes the best vinegar (good vinegars can be just as expensive as good wines) and connoisseurs of vinegar read labels in the same way that wine lovers read wine labels.

Bill and I joined in at the end of a vinegar tasting in one of the trendy delis, where we purchased our picnic lunch. I was astonished by the man giving the demonstration; I've never seen anyone get so excited about vinegar! But I must say I was surprised at how different the samples tasted—I'm sure none of the lovely piquant, vinegars I tried would have done a good job scouring the decks of a British ship!

5 Bread

Most people are familiar with ciabatta and panini, but Italian bakeries also sell cornetti, piadino, michetta, rosetta, biova, ciriola, grissini and pane casareccio, a thick-crusted favourite. In Italy, bread (*pane*) is eaten dipped in oil and vinegar, which is not only healthy but also tasty.

Tuscan sage & olive bread

Serves 4–6

Sponge
250 g (8 oz) unbleached bread flour (sifted)
2 tablespoons yeast
½ teaspoon salt
2 cups (16 fl oz) lukewarm water

Dough
500 g (1 lb) unbleached bread flour
100 g (3½ oz) large green, stuffed olives
1 large bunch sage leaves, roughly torn
1 teaspoon salt
freshly ground black pepper

Preheat oven to 200°C (400°F/Gas Mark 6).
Make the sponge the night before baking. Mix flour with yeast and add salt and water. Stir well to combine and allow sponge to rise in a warm place overnight.

The next morning, place 375 g (12½ oz) flour in a large bowl. Make a well in the centre and add sponge, olives, sage, salt and pepper. Begin to mix the ingredients, adding extra flour as you go. Continue until mixture is very thick and difficult to stir. Tip dough out onto a floured surface and knead for about 10 minutes until smooth and elastic.

Divide bread into two and shape each into an oval shape. Allow bread to rise until doubled in size, then spray with water before baking. Bake for about 1 hour, spraying bread with water every 10 minutes. Allow bread to cool on a wire rack before serving.

Mushroom ciabatta

Makes 2 large oval loaves

10 g (1/3 oz) dried porcini mushrooms
1¾ cups (14 fl oz) warm water
224 g (9 oz) fresh mushrooms, sliced
2 cloves of garlic, crushed
2 tablespoons olive oil
500 g (1 lb) unbleached bread flour
1 tablespoon salt
1 tablespoon granular yeast
cornmeal, for sprinkling

Bland bread

At one time of papal dominance, a high salt tax was imposed. In protest, Tuscan bakers omitted salt. The practice continued out of acquired taste and, as a result, bread is now often eaten with salty cured meats, such as prosciutto, which counteract the bread's blandness.

Preheat oven to 200°C (400°F/Gas Mark 6).

Soak mushrooms in warm water for at least an hour, then drain but reserve liquid. Strain liquid through a cheesecloth two or three times to remove grit, then measure the liquid. Make up to 1½ cups (12 fl oz) with water. Pat porcini mushroom dry, then chop.

Saute fresh mushrooms and garlic in 1 tablespoon of the oil until soft, then raise the heat to high and simmer to reduce the mushroom liquid. Add porcini to mushroom mixture and set aside to cool. In a saucepan, gently warm porcini liquid. Mix flour, salt and yeast together, then add half the mushroom mixture and warmed porcini water. Mix well with a wooden spoon, then turn dough out and knead on a floured surface, adding more flour if necessary to stop the dough sticking. Knead until dough is soft and elastic. Place dough into an oiled bowl and cover with clingwrap. Allow dough to rise for 2 hours, or until it has doubled in size.

Remove dough from the bowl and divide in half. Shape each half into a big, flat oval, then scatter the mushroom mixture over both ovals and roll the dough up, tucking in the ends. Flatten the loaves then roll up again and shape into an oval. The loaves will be compact and quite small, but they will rise quickly.

Place loaves on an oven tray that has been sprinkled with cornmeal. Cover with a dampened tea towel and allow to rise for 2 hours or until doubled in size. Brush loaves with water, then bake for 40 minutes or until golden and crusty. Remove loaves and cool on a wire rack.

Bakers' Guild

A Bakers' Guild, *Collegium Pistorum*, was formed in Rome around 168 BC. The Guild forbade bakers or their children to leave baking and enter other trades, but did provide them with special privileges. However, bakers were forbidden to mix with 'comedians and gladiators' or attend amphitheatre performances lest they were contaminated by the vices of the ordinary people!

Pizza

The main house where Alvina and Umberto live was still a work in progress, as was the summer house and the third villa, and to thank the workmen, Alvina had asked them over for a pizza lunch. One of them, Stefano Santioli, doubles as a chef in a nearby ristorante at night and he had made dough for pizzas marghuerita and spread them out on a marble table near the pizza oven in the garden. The mix of nationalities at lunch reminded us of building our house at Lindfield, which gave rise to my first book *No Sweat Not to Worry She'll be Jake*. Marco, the builder's assistant, is from Albania—23 years old, and too shy to talk to me in his Italian learnt on the job. Pal works for Umberto and Alvina as an estate hand and had done some beautiful stone work. Tom, Marco's father, speaks hardly any Italian and explained that he missed his wife and eight-year-old back home in Albania. Then there was Stefano, the ruddy faced, smiling chef;

Alvina, Umberto, Valter Pierini, Renata Gigliotti, the builder, and his *fidanzata* Clarissa from Russia. Pizzas, salad and little cakes, *dolci*, from Corsini were washed down with chianti, which also washed away earlier inhibitions so that we were soon chatting in broken English, Russian, Albanian, German and Italian. Stefano gave me the recipe for the pizza, which had a very thin crust that I liked. He makes up a dough with flour, olive oil, salt, pepper and yeast and then spreads the pizzas with a tomato salsa, basil, lots of garlic, anchovies and mozzarella.

Later in the week we went for pizza at la Terrazza. And what a pizza—a very thin crust topped with prosciutto, mushrooms, mozzarella, tomatoes, olives, artichokes and salami. The chef, Anna Morra, insisted on taking us into the kitchen to show us how she made the pizzas so crisp and before we knew it we were given complimentary glasses of grappa, too!

I say tomato

To most people, lush vine-ripened tomatoes bring to mind Italian cooking. However, tomatoes, called *pomo d'oro* (golden apple), only appeared in Italy, from Mexico, in 1554. Before then the flavour for many dishes was based on liquamen—a pungent fish sauce.

History of pizza

Legend has it that in 1889 Italy's beloved Queen Marghu
and her husband (another Umberto!) noticed peasants ea
a type of flat topped bread. Queen Marghuerita insisted
trying it and summoned chef Rafaelle Esposito to the palace.
chef baked her a pizza in the colours of the Italian flag—red, g
and white—using tomato, basil and mozzarella. The Queen l
it so much that pizza 'Marghuerita' was named after her.

Artichoke, mozzarella
& salami pizza

Makes 1 large 38–40 cm pizza

Basic pizza dough
1¾ teaspoon active dry yeast,
or 15 g (½ oz) fresh yeast
crumbled pinch of sugar
1⅓ cups (10¾ fl oz) warm water
½ cup (4 fl oz) olive oil
500 g (1 lb) plain (all purpose) flour, sifted
1¼ teaspoons salt

Dissolve yeast and sugar in water in a large mixing bowl. Set aside in a draught-free place for 5 minutes or until foamy. Stir in oil, flour and salt and mix until a rough dough forms. Turn out onto a lightly floured surface and knead for 5 minutes or until dough is soft and satiny. Add more flour if needed. Lightly oil a large bowl then roll dough around to cover surface with oil. Seal bowl with plastic clingwrap and place in a warm draught-free spot for 1½–2 hours or until dough has doubled in volume.

Remove dough from bowl and knead briefly before rolling out onto a floured surface to desired shape. If dough feels too stiff, set aside to rest for a few minutes and start again. Transfer to an oiled pizza pan and finish shaping by hand, forming a slightly raised rim. The dough should be about 5 mm (¼ in) thick. For a thicker crust, cover with a clean tea towel and set aside for 30 minutes to rise again. The pizza is now ready for topping and baking.

Artichoke, mozzarella & salami topping
1 quantity of Basic Pizza Dough rolled onto pizza tray
olive oil, to sprinkle over toppings
3 tablespoons tomato paste
300 g (10 oz) mozzarella cheese, grated
1 × 400 g (13 oz) can of artichoke hearts, drained and thinly sliced lengthways
100 g (3½ oz) Milano salami, thinly sliced
fresh parsley, chopped
fresh oregano, chopped
salt and black pepper to taste

Preheat oven to 200°C (400°F/Gas Mark 6).
Bring dough up at edges to form a slight rim. Brush over with olive oil and then spread pizza base with tomato paste. Cover with mozzarella, salami and slices of artichoke, slightly overlapping on the base until the surface is covered. Sprinkle generously with olive oil and season with black pepper.

Bake for 15 minutes, then reduce heat to 190°C (375°F/Gas Mark 5) and bake for a further 10 minutes or until cheese is bubbling and crust is golden brown. Remove from oven and rest briefly before serving.

Visiting villages

The next morning Bill and I walked under the canopy of overhanging trees, following the walking path that was indicated by painted stripes on the moss-covered rocks, to the medieval hilltop village of Castel del Piano. The village is situated on the slopes of Monte Amiata, an extinct volcano, and the surrounding farmlands, nourished by rich volcanic soil and flowing streams, are renowned for producing superlative olive oil, cheeses, chestnuts, and honey.

We had only been in Tuscany for a few days but people in the village smiled and greeted us with '*Buongiorno*' and '*Come sta signora?*' When we answered '*Molto bene grazie*' we felt like real locals. Italians are the friendliest people. In small villages off the beaten tourist track, such as Castel del Piano, Seggiano, Arcidosso and Cinigiano, people seemed genuinely interested to hear about Australia and were amazed we'd come so far for our annual holiday.

The weekly markets were in full swing and vendors sold colourful fake handbags, tablecloths, handmade lace, leather jackets and tools, while the *porcetta* man did good business with prosciutto, salami and *formaggio* from Pienza. We wandered into a shady vine-covered courtyard where gnarled old men in cloth caps played chess in one corner and two young women chatted animatedly in the other.

Further up the cobbled street we walked past a stone arch with a Latin inscription and chanced upon a pretty trattoria, with red-checked tablecloths and geraniums spilling out of rustic stone pots. We were astonished to find that the main courses cost as little as five to seven euro, so we took a table for two and dined alfresco. There had been some light rain through the night and the piazza was fresh and sparkling in the thin autumn sunshine. Around the fountain, pigeons flapped and fought over scraps of food.

We sat, soaking up the ambience and watching mammas, baskets over their arms, shopping and chatting. Nonnas pushed beautifully dressed grandchildren in strollers, and men in the café opposite sat sipping cappuccini and debating politics. People milled around, creating that bustling atmosphere common in Europe in the late morning when people are hurrying home to prepare the midday meal for their family.

Sharp at midday, church bells chime and chained metal doors clank as they're yanked down from above, slid over or slammed to. The clanging echoes around the village signalling that morning shopping has ended and siesta is about to begin.

Lunch is not eaten at desks or on the run, but is a main meal and may consist of a hearty soup followed by pasta or a meat dish and washed down with a carafe

of local vino. Siesta follows and entire villages slumber for 2–3 hours while their inhabitants rest before returning to their workplaces at around 3 pm. Most stores don't close until 7 or 8 at night, but arriving in a village during the somnolent siesta time can be a problem if you're planning to go to the post office, the bank or the *tabaccàio* to buy a train ticket.

After lunch we wandered further up the road to Corsini, a shop famous for its sweet delicacies and cakes. Behind the glass counter displays stood Signora Corsini, who insisted on giving me some delicious lemon peel dipped in chocolate to take home. Alvina had told us about Corsini's *glacé marrone*, the most delicious chestnut poached in sugar syrup that turns into a light honey which melts in the mouth. They are usually eaten after dinner, but the aroma coming out of the box was too much, so we polished them off on our walk, licking the honey off our fingers.

I always thought 'honey was just honey', but in nearby Seggiano, acacia, eucalyptus, sunflower, honeydew, chestnut wildflower and acacia honeys are produced. These honeys in the Seggiano range come from the hives of the local beekeeper, teacher and biologist, Mauro Pagliacci (top left), who keeps some 500 bee families and moves them around to different locations according to the particular flowering season. I adored the chestnut honey, which has a hint of sophisticated bitterness that the Italians call *amaro*.

Later that day, I was off to an appointment with the local hairdresser. Lorenzo, the stylist (top right), was determined to practise his English on me. He told me he had lived and worked in Rome for 20 years and

O Sole Mio

Che bella cosa na jurnata 'e sole, n'aria serena doppa na tempesta! Pe' ll'aria fresca pare gia' na festa
Che bella cosa na jurnata 'e sole.

Ma n'atu sole
cchiu' bello, oi ne'.
'O sole mio
sta 'nfronte a te!
'O sole, 'o sole mio
sta 'nfronte a te
sta 'nfronte a te!

Lucene 'e llastre d'a fenesta toia;
'na lavaannara canta e se ne vanta
e pe' tramente torce, spanne e canta
lucene 'e llastre d'a fenesta toia.

Ma n'atu sole
cchiu' bello, oi ne'.
'O sole mio
sta 'nfronte a te!
'O sole, 'o sole mio
sta 'nfronte a te,
sta 'nfronte a te!

had lots of English and American clients. We managed with a combination of his English and my Italian and although the blow dry took an hour and a half, the fact that he sang *O Sole Mio* and other operatic arias the entire time made it pass very quickly. I was relieved he didn't wash my hair with olive oil, like they used to do in ancient Pompeii!

Afterwards, Bill and I walked home down the steep, chestnut-lined road, which was partially hidden by a misty drizzle of rain. I was looking forward to a glass of good red and the tomato and cheese tarts we'd seen Alvina making that morning followed by a mid-afternoon siesta.

Smoked salmon carpaccio
with oil & lemon

Serves 4

¼ cup (2 fl oz) extra virgin olive oil

3 tablespoons lemon juice

1 small red (Spanish) onion, finely chopped

2 teaspoons small whole capers

350 g (11 oz) smoked salmon, allow 3–4 slices per person

1 tablespoon fresh parsley, roughly chopped

freshly ground black pepper to taste

capers, extra, for garnish

Combine oil, lemon juice, onion and capers in a bowl and whisk. Arrange smoked salmon on serving plates.
Drizzle dressing over smoked salmon, sprinkle with parsley and pepper and serve. Garnish with extra capers.

Mediterranean tomato & cheese tarts

Makes 12

3 sheets filo pastry, thawed

½ cup (1 oz) soft breadcrumbs

2 cups (10 oz) Edam cheese, grated

2 small tomatoes, sliced

salt and freshly ground black pepper

fresh basil leaves, roughly torn

Preheat oven to 200°C (400°F/Gas Mark 6).

Place one sheet of pastry on a large chopping board. Sprinkle over half the breadcrumbs.

Top with another sheet of pastry. Repeat breadcrumbs and top with last sheet of pastry.

Cut filo into ten 9 cm (3½ in) squares.

 Place each layered square in a greased patty tin, twisting each layer so the corners don't line up.

Divide cheese among the pastry cases. Cut tomato slices in half and arrange 2 pieces on top of the cheese.

Sprinkle with salt and pepper. Bake pastry cases for 12–15 minutes or until pastry is cooked and golden.

Remove from oven. Cool slightly. Place on a serving dish, sprinkle over basil leaves, and serve.

Sunset serenity

The evenings are mild at Alvina and Umberto's and we spent one relaxing with a bottle of excellent Antinori from Orvieto and nibbling on *parmigiano reggiano* and fresh figs.

The pink blush of sunset slowly sank beneath hills green with newly planted vines; behind them, the peak of Monte Amiata stood silhouetted proudly against the horizon.

The air was still, but the tree tops swayed in a gentle breeze. The only sound was the muted chirp of crickets. I felt very relaxed, which is a not a state that I manage to achieve very often.

Bill and Umberto cooked Tuscan chicken, which thankfully took care of itself, because Bill had soon nodded off beside me! After dinner, which the boys served up with a great flourish (very macho!) we sat by the fire, listening to Verdi, sipping Sambuca Galliano and reminiscing.

Horace ode 1.9

Horace was one of ancient Rome's most celebrated poets. This version of his ode 1.9 was translated by the first Corpus professor of Latin at Oxford University, John Conington.

O, ask not what the morn will bring,
But count as gain each day
that chance may give you;
Sport in life's young spring,
Nor scorn sweet love,
nor merry dance,
While years are green,
while sullen eld,
is distant.
Now the walk, the game,
The whispered talk at sunset held,
Each in its hour prefer their claim.

Cooking class

In the last four decades, much of the Italian countryside has undergone a metamorphosis as many people who were unable to make a living off the land moved to the cities. For those who stayed, the problem of making the farm a viable proposition remained.

In many cases, families vacated their old stone farmhouses, selling them to members of the up-and-coming middle class, or to foreigners. This injection of money has given the countryside a new lease on life—vineyards and olive groves were planted, fruit trees pruned, wells and stone fences repaired, gardens laid out, homes rebuilt and restored (often to more than their former glory) and garages and roads constructed.

Many of these villas are rented by people escaping city life, some are weekenders and some are devoted to *agriturismo*—agriculture tourism where the owners work the land, tend to their livestock and have paying guests. While *agriturismo* may have started out as a means to make ends meet, it has actually blossomed into a thriving industry.

Much of the traditional farming way of life may have changed, but the slow rich rhythm of life in the Italian countryside remains.

Many of the homestays involve the guests in the daily routine—olive oil production, making bread and cheese, grape picking, bottling the fruits grown on the farm and making traditional handicrafts.

Alvina and Umberto took us to visit their friends, Yves Pagni and Peggy Spalinger at Casa Pagni, an *agriturismo* of another kind. Yves is a chef who, in addition to cooking superb meals for their intimate ristorante, gives lessons on Italian cooking. Peggy is a talented jewellery designer. We had a wonderful day with them and their toddler Jeremy.

The villa was beautifully decorated by Peggy with rainbow colours and beds with crisp white coverlets trimmed with lace and stacked high with soft, fluffy pillows. Fresh flowers in every room filled the villa with fragrance, which blended with the aroma of Yves' mouth-watering cooking.

I could hear my stomach rumbling and hoped Yves had chosen simple recipes so that we could eat soon. We sat in front of the crackling fire, drinking wine from large glasses and feeling more relaxed by the minute. I almost forgot we were there to learn to cook!

The kitchen was small and spotless, filled with knives, whisks, mixing bowls and pots and pans. Stone urns, spilling basil and rosemary, stood on an ancient timber shelf above marble benches. Delicious aromas wafted from a huge frying pan where onions and garlic sizzled in golden-green olive oil. In another pan, *pancetta*, a type of Italian bacon, was simmering in chicken stock. I was relieved to see no sign of donkey meat, a dish I'd noticed on menus in restaurants (I couldn't have looked Cosimo or Concetta in the eye the next day).

Yves is passionate about Italian food and even more passionate about helping people like me cook dishes that are delicious but quick and easy. By the time we'd put our aprons on, Yves had refilled our large wine glasses and I knew this was a lesson I was going to enjoy.

We cooked cannelloni, pork and wild pear jam, served on a bed of artichokes. Dessert was ricotta cheese served with three homemade jams and local Seggiano honey. Yves told us that serving honey with strong cheese balances out the flavour. The meal was followed by hot chestnuts roasted in the oven, a glass of wine and plenty of good conversation and company.

Tomato & calamari soup

Yves gave me this very tasty recipe, which is very simple.
Serves 4
600 g of small calamari
2 cloves of garlic
1 teaspoon grated lemon rind
20 g chopped parsley

300 g of peeled ripe tomatoes, cubed
100 ml red wine
100 ml of water
olive oil, salt and pepper
4 slices of bread

Clean the calamari, including the head and cut into small slices. Pour the olive oil into a frying pan and fry the garlic. When it starts to colour, add the lemon rind, parsley and calamari and cook for two minutes.

Add the tomatoes and keep cooking for another two minutes. Add the wine and water and cook for a further 10 minutes. Add salt and pepper to taste.

Serve on a plate on top of slices of bread that have been roasted and lightly drizzled with olive oil.

Veal rolls with celery & gorgonzola

The combination of meat and cheese in this recipe from Yves Pagni is delicious.

Serves 4

3 long celery strips
12 small slices of very thin veal
100 ml white wine
3L of broth
150 g gorgonzola cheese
salt, pepper, flour and olive oil

Cut the celery to make 12 little sticks and roll them in the veal. Hold together with a toothpick.
   Lightly flour and fry in oil in the saucepan for a few minutes. Then add the white wine and cook for a further two minutes. Add the broth, gorgonzola and salt and pepper to taste. Simmer for 40 minutes.
   The sauce should be slightly thick. This meal goes well with boiled potatoes and vegetables.

Rack of veal with thyme
on garlic mashed potato

Serves 4

½ cup (4 fl oz) olive oil

1 kg (2 lb) rack of veal with 8 points

2 tablespoons roasted garlic puree

2 tablespoons thyme leaves

salt and freshly ground black pepper

1¼ cups (10 fl oz) white wine

1¼ cups (10 fl oz) veal or chicken stock

750 g (1½ lb) potatoes, peeled and chopped

2 tablespoons olive oil

1 tablespoon capers, chopped

Preheat oven to 180°C (350°F/Gas Mark 4).
Heat olive oil in a pan and brown the veal on both sides until well sealed. This will take almost 5 minutes. Remove veal from the pan and place on a rack in a baking dish. Rub 1 tablespoon roasted garlic and 1 tablespoon of thyme leaves. Season with salt and pepper.

Add half the wine and stock to the baking dish. Roast in the oven for 20 minutes or until veal is cooked to your liking then wrap in foil and leave to rest for 10 minutes.

Boil potatoes until soft. Drain, then mash (or puree) and add olive oil, chopped capers and the other half of the roasted garlic. Mix well and season with salt and pepper.

Add the remaining stock, wine and thyme to the veal pan juices and cook over a medium heat for 5 minutes or until the liquid has reduced by a third.

Serve veal on a bed of mashed potatoes and drizzle over pan juices. Garnish with thyme leaves.

Penne with herbs
& parmesan

Yves Pagni also taught us how to make this lovely aromatic pasta.

Serves 4

2 cloves of garlic, squeezed
300 g of ripe, peeled, cubed tomatoes
20 g of fresh mixed herbs (sage, thyme, marjoram, oregano and mint)
350 g of penne
100 g of shaved parmesan
salt, pepper and olive oil

Fry the squeezed garlic in a frying pan, add the tomatoes and cook for two minutes. Add the chopped herbs and leave for one minute. Turn off the heat and add salt and pepper to taste.

Cook the pasta separately in plenty of salted water, and drain. Turn the heat on and heat the sauce until hot then add the cooked, drained pasta to the sauce. Shake for a minute or two until the sauce is mixed through.

Serve with extra parmesan shavings.

Nice neighbours

Alvina and Umberto's neighbours, Santina and Fernando Gianelli, use their land in typical Italian style. We drove along the narrow chestnut-lined roads edged with lavender and wildflowers to their sprawling two-storey stone farmhouse. Below the main house stood neat rows of flourishing grape vines, often with a rose bush planted at one end. Rose bushes are the 'canaries' of vignerons, indicating the state of the soil.

Olive groves grew nearby and farmyards beside them housed an assortment of animals: rabbits, pigs, peacocks, chickens, cows and ducks.

Santina came out to meet us, smiling broadly and wiping her hands on her apron before giving me a kiss on each cheek and a huge hug. We hadn't met before but it was as if she were greeting an old friend. Fernando was behind her, shaking Bill's hand. Their daughter Clara and sixteen-year-old grandson Luca stood smiling shyly. We sat around the wooden table in the huge kitchen, which was warm and filled with the aroma of bean soup and freshly baked bread.

Visiting them was like taking a step into another world—a slower, simpler, uncomplicated world where life adjusted to the pace of nature. We strolled down to an area under the house where, at a long wooden table, Santina sits and sorts chestnuts by hand. It is painstaking work. As she chatted animatedly about her life, her hands flew over the chestnuts, separating those for sale from those for the animals.

At the rear of the room, a spacious cellar was packed with shelves laden with preserves: hazelnuts, walnuts, cheese, honey, sun-dried tomatoes, quinces, pears, cherries and apples. Two vats of olive oil stood in the corner. Even the wine was made from their own grapes. Alvina had mentioned that Santina's pecorino cheese was the best in Tuscany. She makes it in the morning, using the whey to make ricotta in the afternoon. Santina seemed bemused that I found her daily chores so interesting.

'How do you make your pecorino?' I asked.

'In a bowl. How do you make yours?' she answered earnestly. Cheese-making was so much a part of her life, as it had been for her mother and her grandmother, and now her daughter, that she couldn't imagine I didn't make my own. Bill raise his eyebrows, but he didn't comment.

Luca was keen to show us his menagerie, so we walked along a path between gnarled old fruit trees, rusty with the hues of autumn, to see the cows and pigs. I wondered what our bank manager's reaction would be if we told him we wanted to buy our own villa in Tuscany.

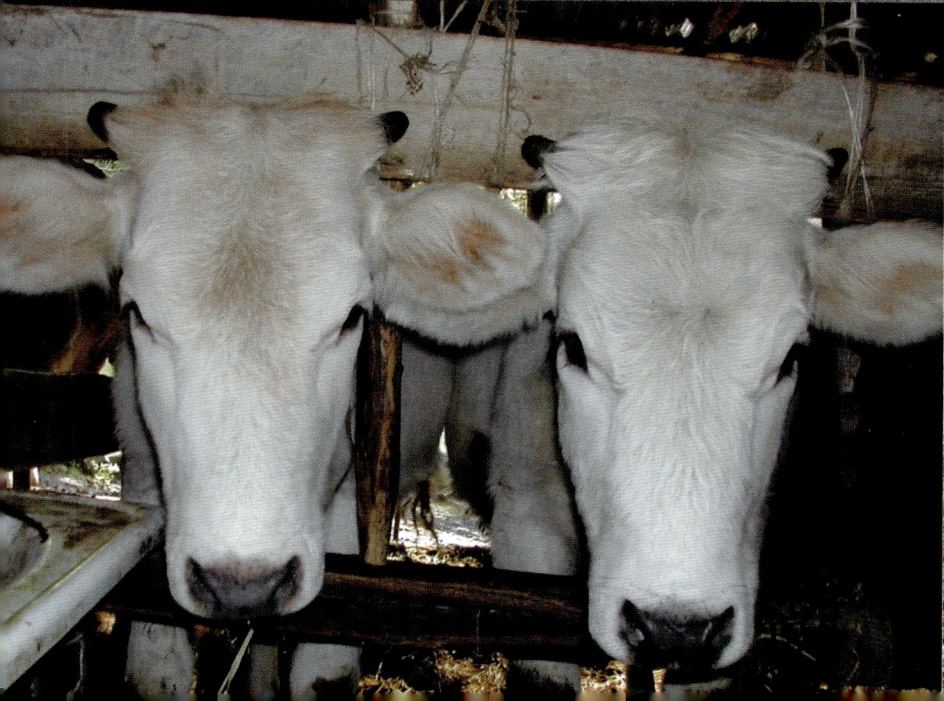

Chestnut soup

Serves 4

2 teaspoons of olive oil
½ medium onion, finely chopped
1 carrot, sliced
1 celery stalk, sliced
4 cups of chicken stock
1 teaspoon of sugar
1 bay leaf
¼ teaspoon basil leaves
⅛ teaspoon of marjoram leaves
about 24 chestnuts (roasted and skinned), or 1 tin chestnut puree.
½ cup of milk or cream
¾ cup of Marsala or sherry
salt and pepper to taste

In a large pot, heat the oil and sauté the onion, carrot and celery. Add the chicken broth, sugar, bay leaf, basil, marjoram and chestnuts. Simmer for about 25 minutes, or until the chestnuts are tender, then remove and discard the bay leaf.

Transfer to a food processor or blender and pureé. Once smooth, return to the pot and stir in the milk or cream. Bring to a gentle boil. Add the Marsala or sherry and season to taste with salt and pepper. Serve hot or cold.

Note: If you are roasting chestnuts, make a small slit in the shell, so the chestnuts do not explode.

Cheese

Italy has a huge range of cheese (*formaggio*)—I counted over 25 varieties in one tiny cheese shop we visited. Apart from being eaten raw, cheese is important in Italian cooking. Chefs sprinkle it generously over soups or pasta, shave it into paper-thin slices for salads or garnish, grate it for stuffing pasta or flavouring creamy sauces for lasagna—even roast it!

Desserts are often cheese sweetened or with grape, sugar or honey. In Rome, we feasted on figs filled with Sambuca-flavoured mascarpone, a type of creamy dessert cheese.

The 'king' of Italian cheeses, parmigiano reggiano, was documented as far back as the Middle Ages. When the region south of the Po Valley was under the rule of seven different countries, parmigiano was known as the 'great cheese of seven countries', and the formula remained unchanged throughout 700 years of history! Herdsmen driving sheep, cattle and goats to the lush, cooler pastures in the hills and mountains are credited with the discovery that milk could be transformed into cheese—a solid food that could be stored for months, and, even better, often improved with age.

Climate and geography control which cheeses are be produced. Cow's milk cheese, such as crescenza and fontina, is more commonly found in the north, while the south's sparser vegetation is more suited to goats and sheep and produces pecorino and caprini.

Cheese will have a different colour, odour, flavour, even texture, depending on the technique and the season. Cheese made in the spring can taste quite different to that made in autumn. Taste is enhanced by herbs and spices, such as saffron or peppercorn.

Ageing is important. Some cheeses, like gorgonzola, are best eaten fresh; others, like bel paese (beautiful country), are tastier after maturing for months.

Mozzarella di bufala campagna is a unique cheese made by the *pas filata* process, where the curd is dipped into hot whey before being stretched and kneaded to the right consistency. Traditionally made from the milk of the water buffalo, today it is more often made from cows' milk.

While regular mozzarella is best known for topping pizzas, fresh mozzarella packed in whey or water is absolutely delicious eaten alone or with a drizzle of olive oil and some freshly ground black pepper.

Bocconcini, miniature mozzarella balls, are often marinated in olive oil or herbs and are delicious with tomato and fresh basil as a starter. For those whose waistline is past redemption, there's always *manteca*—mozzarella wrapped around a dob of butter!

FONTINA ORIGINALE al KG € 15⁵⁰

SPECK DOLCISSIMO al Kg € 18⁰⁸

...TINA al Kg €...

...TIROLO MAGRO Kg € 13³⁹

PECORI NERA al KG € 13⁴³

EURO ...NO € 16⁵³

PECORINO DI PIE... Pecmiaio M... al Kg € 15...

...TUTTI ...OLPA ...ori in finissimi pezzi ...VISTA ...OLPA COSI... ...DO ITALIANO

Pecorino FRESCO € 10,20 al Kg

Pecorino SEMI-STAGIONATO (senza conservanti) € 11,90 al Kg

Green beans with prosciutto,
parmesan, and quail eggs

Serves 4

6 quail eggs
250 g (8 oz) green beans, blanched
50 g (1⅔ oz) prosciutto slices
parmesan cheese, shaved
freshly ground black pepper to taste
sea salt to taste

Dressing
2 tablespoons extra virgin olive oil
1 tablespoon white wine vinegar

Place quail eggs in a small saucepan of cold water, bring to the boil and cook for 3 minutes. Rinse under cold water until eggs are cool, then peel and cut in half.

Combine beans, prosciutto, quail eggs and parmesan cheese in a bowl. Sprinkle with black pepper and sea salt. Drizzle dressing over dish and serve.

On our way

We bade farewell to our hosts and headed towards Siena to continue our Tuscan tour.

After half an hour of driving down lanes bordered with golden-hued trees, we came to a halt in a narrow lane where a young shepherd herded his flock past cars and motorbikes that had slowed to a crawl. Aside from the traffic, it could have been a scene from hundreds of years ago, until we looked more closely at the shepherd—an incongruous sight in bright white, modern running shoes with music blaring from his earphones as he sang loudly (and out of tune) in English!

This road passes some of Italy's most beautiful scenery. Many of the houses we passed on the road had rich orange pumpkins perched on their balconies as they prepared for Halloween.

We soon stopped on a grassy verge, spread out our picnic rug and enjoyed asparagus with pecorino and pancetta we had bought at the *alimentari* at Castel del Piano.

There wasn't a cloud in the sky and the only thing that made us get back in the car was knowing that Siena was just an hour's drive away.

Asparagus with pecorino
& pancetta

Serves 4–6

500 g (1 lb) asparagus
juice of 1 lemon
100 ml (3 fl oz) extra virgin olive oil
salt and freshly ground black pepper to taste
8 thin slices pancetta, cut into pieces
1 cup (2 ½ oz) pecorino, shaved

Trim off the thick asparagus ends and cook asparagus in boiling water for 4 minutes until slightly tender. Run under cold water until asparagus is cool, then dry on paper towel.

   For the dressing, place lemon juice in a bowl and slowly add oil, whisking until dressing is thick. Season with salt and pepper.

   Pour dressing over asparagus and serve with pancetta and shavings of pecorino cheese.

Siena

Siena is one of the most gracious cities in Italy. *'T Cor magis tibi Siena pandit'* (Siena opens its heart for you) is the city's motto and Siena feels open and harmonious in every way. Perhaps it's because Siena is smaller (with a population of around 60 000) or perhaps it's because of Siena's beautiful Piazza del Campo—a huge-fan-shaped area where people sit reading, sketching, or snoozing in the sun, but Siena has retained its medieval atmosphere, reflecting the golden age of art and trade that it once enjoyed.

The city was originally an Etruscan settlement that became a self-governing city in the twelfth century. The rival city of Florence was determined to conquer Siena and, weakened by party strife and civic turmoil, the Sienese accepted French assistance to save them from attacks by Spain and Cosimo I de Medici. Under attack, the Sienese fled to the summit-top village of Montalcino, where they held out for some time, but were later starved into surrender and governed by the Spanish until 1557, when the town of Siena was sold to Cosimo de Medici.

The countryside south of Siena represents the best of Tuscany. Gentle rounded hills with orderly lines of vineyards or verdant cypress trees winding up to farmhouses and quaint fortressed villages high on the hills are postcard perfect. Silvery grey olive groves and grazing sheep dot the hills. We had been to Siena before on tours with the Dante Alighieri Society and the David Lowe Sculpture group, so as soon as we arrived Bill and I visited our favourite café on the Piazza del Campo, Bar il Palio. I had Tuscan bean soup with a chunk of crusty bread, to which I added my own dob of Alvina's homemade pear and tomato chutney, and Bill ordered grilled eggplant with pork mince ragout. We sat in the warm sunshine watching tourists and locals share the square with fluttering pigeons.

City of legends

In Roman legend, the city of Siena was founded by Senius and Aschius, the sons of Remus, who stole a statue of a she-wolf from the temple of Apollo and took her to found their own city, giving Siena the emblem of the wolf and the symbolic colours of their own horses, one black and one white.

In reality, Siena was already occupied by the Etruscans, but the Romans later made it a military colony between 27–40 BC.

Homemade pear
& tomato chutney

Alvina's chutney is perfect with chunky bread and Santina's pecorino cheese

1¼ cups of roughly chopped tomatoes, fresh or canned
(remove the skins if using fresh tomatoes)
1¼ cups pears, diced fresh or canned (remove skins
from fresh pears)
¼ cup of raisins
¼ cup chopped green pepper
¼ cup chopped onion
½ cup of sugar
¼ cup of white vinegar
½ teaspoon salt

¼ teaspoon each of ground ginger
¼ teaspoon of dry mustard
dash of cayenne pepper
1 tablespoon of chopped canned pimento (capsicum)

Combine all ingredients except pimento. Bring to the boil and boil gently, stirring frequently until the mixture thickens and reduces. This takes about 1 hour.

Add pimiento and boil for another 5 minutes. Put the hot chutney into clean, hot jars and fill to the top. Seal.

Grilled eggplant
with pork mince ragout

Serves 4

1 tablespoon olive oil
1 onion, finely chopped
2 gloves of garlic, finely chopped
170 g (6 oz) minced pork
¾ cup of chopped tomatoes
2 medium zucchinis, finely chopped
1 tablespoon fresh sage, chopped
2 large eggplants, sliced 1 cm thick
mozzarella cheese

Heat oil in a large heavy-based frying pan and fry the onion and garlic for 3–5 minutes, until softened. Add pork mince and cook for 5 minutes, stirring lightly until pork browns.

Then add chopped zucchini, chopped tomatoes and sage. Cook for a further 3–5 minutes until zucchini softens.

Slice the eggplants into thick 1 cm slices and drizzle with a little more olive oil. Dry fry them on a hotplate or place them under a grill for around 4 minutes. Once browned, place the eggplant slices on a plate and top with a few large tablespoons of the pork mixture and a 1 cm slice of mozzarella.

Place back under the grill briefly, or in the oven until the cheese melts and browns slightly.

Alvina serves this with a salad of bitter leaves topped with an oil and vinegar dressing, along with still-warm homemade bread and a glass of Ruffino Chianti Classico.

Chicken Marsala

Serves 4

4 large chicken breast fillets, pounded
seasoned flour
30 g (1 oz) butter
2 tablespoons olive oil
¾ cup (6 fl oz) dry Marsala
¼ cup (2 fl oz) chicken stock
30 g (1 oz) butter, softened
freshly ground black pepper to taste

Coat chicken in flour and shake off excess. Heat butter and oil in a frying pan until butter is foaming. Add chicken and cook for 3 minutes each side. Stir in Marsala, bring to the boil and simmer for 15 minutes, or until chicken is cooked.

Remove chicken and set aside to keep warm. Add stock, bring to the boil and cook for 2 minutes. Whisk in softened butter and season to taste with black pepper. To serve, spoon sauce over chicken.

Things to do

- Marvel at Siena's spectacular gothic cathedral, dating from 1215.
- Visit Palazza Pubblico, the impressive town hall on the Piazza del Campo, where you can be inspired by Sienese frescoes in the Museo Civico or climb the bell tower.
- Explore the artwork in the Museo dell'Opera Metropolitana, next to the cathedral.
- Join in the fun of Palio if you are in Siena in July and August, but be sure to book accommodation early for this busy time of year. The nearby village of Castel del Piano also has a much smaller palio race, which is held in September.

Il Palio

Tuscany's largest and most well-known festival, Palio, is a bareback horse race held in Siena twice yearly in July and August. The race, dating from 1283, allows jockeys from the city's 17 districts (*contrade*) to vie for the prize of a silk banner (*palio*). Each district has its own colours and allegiances. Festivities include pageants, processions and heavy gambling.

Tuscan bean soup

Serves 4

4 cups (6 oz) green beans, trimmed
2 cloves of garlic
2 tablespoons olive oil
I onion, finely chopped
3 sticks celery, sliced
I leek, sliced
2 carrots, peeled and chopped
190 g (6 oz) tomato paste
I x 400 g (13 oz) can tomatoes
2 cups (8 fl oz) beef stock or water
I teaspoon dried thyme
125g (4 oz) spinach, washed
salt and freshly ground black pepper

Cook beans in boiling water until just tender. While beans are cooking, crush garlic and mash with the salt.

Heat oil in a large saucepan. Add garlic mixture, onion, celery, leek and carrot. Cover and cook, shaking the pan frequently, until vegetables are golden. Stir in tomato paste, tomatoes with their juice, stock or water and thyme. Bring to the boil, cover and cook gently for 45 minutes.

Drain beans reserving half a cup of the liquid. Put the beans into a blender or food processor with reserved liquid and process until very finely chopped. Add chopped beans and spinach to the soup and cook for 5 minutes. Season with salt and pepper and serve with crusty Italian bread.

Superb sculpture

I'm always astonished at how the Italians go about their business apparently oblivious to the artistic wonders surrounding them. Our enthusiastic guide on the sculpture tour, Dante, led us through narrow streets lined with stone buildings boasting sculptures and gargoyles. Bill and I gasped and gazed while cameras clicked every few seconds. We became more excited by the minute as buildings were named, histories given, myths related and the lives and works of the architects, painters or sculptors described in detail. The wide, open piazzas pay homage to Italian heroes, politicians and religious figures—the Madonna, especially, gazes serenely down from many plinths, a constant reminder of Italy's Catholicism. Every corner reveales tiny shrines festooned with fresh flowers.

Over a light lunch of risotto and frittata (and a couple of glasses of local vino) we marvelled again at Italian ingenuity. Like the Greeks, the Romans created most of their sculptures in marble; many were so realistic that I fully expected the eyelashes to flutter on the often life-size figures!

Frittata with roast pumpkin,
potato & rosemary

Serves 12

300 g (10 oz) butternut pumpkin, diced into 2 cm (¾ in) pieces
220 g (7 oz) potatoes, peeled and diced
220 g (7 oz) sweet potato, peeled and diced into 2 cm (¾ in) pieces
1 tablespoon olive oil
2 sprigs rosemary, roughly chopped
½ teaspoon sea salt
4 eggs
½ cup (4 fl oz) milk
1 clove of garlic, crushed
½ cup parmesan cheese, grated
salt and freshly ground black pepper

Place pumpkin, potato, sweet potato, oil, 1 sprig of rosemary and sea salt in a baking dish. Mix together and bake for 20 minutes or until just cooked.

Grease a 12 cup muffin tin and line it with paper. In a bowl, mix together eggs, milk, garlic, cheese, remaining rosemary, salt and pepper.

Add potato, pumpkin and sweet potato. Pour into muffin cups, reduce oven temperature to 180°C (350°F/Gas Mark 4) and bake for 30–35 minutes. Serve hot.

Risotto with baby spinach
& gorgonzola

1 L (32 fl oz) chicken stock
2 tablespoons olive oil
2 cloves of crushed garlic
1 finely chopped onion
2 cups (14 oz) Arborio rice
½ cup (4 fl oz) white wine
1 tablespoon butter
220 g (7 oz) baby spinach
220g (7 oz) gorgonzola cheese, cubed
salt and freshly ground black pepper

Place stock in a saucepan and bring to the boil. Leave simmering.

Heal oil in a large saucepan, add garlic and onion, and cook for 5 minutes, or until soft.

Add rice, and stir until well coated.

Pour in wine and cook, until liquid has been absorbed. Add stock, a ladle at a time, stirring continuously until liquid has been absorbed, before adding the next ladle of stock. Keep adding stock this way and stirring until all stock is used and until rice is cooked but still a little firm to bite. Add 1 tablespoon of butter to finish.

Add spinach, cheese and seasonings. Stir and cook until spinach is just wilted and cheese has melted. Serve immediately.

Portofino

Leaving Siena behind, we headed north-west through the hilly hinterland towards the gleaming Ligurian coast, widely known as the Italian Riviera. The area was once ruled by Saracens, Lombards, Venetians and Greeks—a rich history that is reflected in the cuisine of the region, which is based on seafood, olives, anchovies, flat bread, soups and oils.

Our first stop was the pretty fishing village and resort town of Portofino, which clings to the cliffside above a harbour dotted with colourful bobbing boats. The hills are emerald with groves of olives, cypress and pines, and the ridges, especially of Monte Portofino, are the perfect vantage point for views across the pale-pink adobe houses to the Mediterranean beyond.

Car traffic is restricted on the steep cliffs and tiny roads and Portofino gets very busy in the high season, but once we made it down to the scenic Piazzetta by the harbour, which is fringed with restaurants and cafes, we found a serene spot to while away the afternoon.

Afterwards we wandered the bougainvillea-tangled streets past lavish houses and the famed Hotel Splendido, once a monastry.

Portofino has excellent boutique shopping and a number of medieval attractions, such as Castello Brown, a seventeenth-century fortress that dominates the port and takes its name from the British consul who bought it in 1867. The region around the town is a protected park and the seabed is a *riserva marina*, a marine reserve that shelters corals, sponges and many species of sea creatures.

Changing hands

Situated on the Liguarian coast about 40 kilometre east of Genoa is Portofino, in an area once ruled by the Greeks, Romans, Saracens, Lombards, Venetians and French. This small but glamorous seaside resort was already famous in ancient times when it belonged to the Benedictine Abbey of San Fruttusosa di Capodimonte in the tenth century before passing in 1171 to the Rapalla jurisdiction. It grew to be a haunt for bohemian artists and writers, but is now an elegant and sophisticated resort frequented by the international jet set, who entertain one another in their superb yachts moored along the waterfront.

Marvellous 7 Markets

Everywhere we went in Italy, stalls and markets provided a visual delight, with a spectrum of colour glinting from fruit and vegetable stalls, fish mongers, tiny *supermercati*, delicatessens, butcher shops, boutiques and street stalls.

In the resort towns of Sorrento, Portofino, Cinque Terre and Positano, many boutiques stock designer labels, but that's not to say you're not tempted by colourful displays of sandals, sarongs, handmade jewellery, hand-wrought leather belts, ceramic and porcelain figurines and bright, flowing cheesecloth kaftans at street vendors.

Even more tempting are the fresh fruits resting beside gourmet oils, high quality vinegars and Italian alcoholic drinks such as Limoncello and Vin Santo. We spent hours browsing the supermarkets and stalls, reading the Italian labels and marvelling at the wonderful variety of delicacies. Looking at all the food made us hungry again, so we found a small trattoria which specialised in chicken with anchovy sauce.

Tomato, bocconcini & basil salad

Serves 4–6

410 g (13 oz) Roma tomatoes, thickly sliced
250 g (4 oz) bocconcini, sliced
½ cup (1 oz) fresh basil leaves, shredded
extra virgin olive oil
dash of balsamic vinegar
sea salt and freshly ground black pepper to taste
crusty bread, for serving

Arrange tomatoes, bocconcini and basil leaves on individual plates. Drizzle with extra virgin olive oil and balsamic vinegar and sprinkle with sea salt and freshly ground black pepper. Serve with warm crusty bread.

Chicken with anchovy sauce

Serves 4

1.5 kg (3 lb) chicken, jointed
1½ tablespoons olive oil
1 small onion, finely chopped
1 clove garlic, finely chopped
½ cup (4 fl oz) dry white wine
1½ tablespoons white wine vinegar
1 cup (4 fl oz) chicken stock
½ teaspoon dried oregano
1 bay leaf
1 tablespoon black olives, pitted and finely sliced
3 flat anchovy fillets, rinsed in cold water, dried and chopped
2 tablespoons fresh parsley, chopped
freshly ground black pepper to taste

Wash chicken under cold running water then pat dry with kitchen towel. Season to taste with black pepper. Heat oil in a heavy-based frying pan and cook chicken a few pieces at a time until brown on both sides. Remove from pan and set aside. Drain off pan juices and discard.

Add onion and garlic to pan and cook, stirring constantly for 5 minutes or until lightly browned. Stir in wine and vinegar, bring to the boil and simmer until reduced to 3 tablespoons. Pour in chicken stock and boil, stirring constantly for 2 minutes. Return chicken to the pan, add oregano and bay leaf. Bring to the boil, cover and simmer for 30 minutes until tender. Remove chicken pieces from pan and set aside to keep warm. Remove and discard bay leaf. Bring stock to the boil and boil until slightly thickened.

Stir in olives, anchovies and parsley and cook for 1 minute longer, then spoon over chicken. Serve.

Crispy duck with blueberry
vinegar & zucchini flowers

Serves 4

2 tablespoons sunflower oil

4 duck breasts, skin on

3 tablespoons balsamic vinegar

freshly ground black pepper

¼ teaspoon ground cinnamon

4 tablespoons fresh blueberries

12 zucchini flowers

90 g (3 oz) plain flour

1 cup (8 fl oz) water

oil for cooking

Heat oil in a frying pan and cook duck, skin side down over a low heat until skin is golden. Turn and cook on other side.

Add vinegar, black pepper, cinnamon and blueberries. Cover and cook over a low heat for 15 minutes or until duck is tender.

To prepare zucchini flowers, gradually sift flour into water and mix with a fork until batter is smooth. If necessary, add more water. Pour 2.5 cm (1 in) oil into a frying pan and heat until very hot. Dip flowers into the batter and cook a few at a time until golden.

To serve, arrange duck and flowers on a serving plate and spoon blueberry sauce over duck.

Please note: Although blueberries have been used in this recipe, any berry fruit may be substituted.

Cinque Terre

Nestled along the sheer coastline of the Ligurian coast and just a short distance apart are the five picturesque little villages of Cinque Terre. Brightly painted houses perch precariously on the hillside, as if they might tumble into the sea at any moment. Hiking between the towns is popular but tiring, as old donkey trails lead up and down the cliffs up to 1000 feet above sea level.

We visited Riomaggiore by ferry and walked to nearby Manarola. Each of the five villages has its own unique character and all seem virtually untouched by the passage of time.

The famed Cinque Terre white wine is produced here, and vines ramble over the hills, covering over 5000 acres and supported on the steep incline by approximately 4200 miles of hand-built sandstone walls. It is this feat of perseverance, against the odds of gravity, that has seen Cinque Terre declared a UNESCO World Heritage Site.

Cuisine in Cinque Terre is simple but flavoursome and includes toffie, a pasta made from chestnut flour.

Pesto, credited to nearby Genoa, is popular and the locally grown, early spring ingredients of artichokes, zucchini, Swiss chard, leeks and potatoes are made into a variety of pies and frittata (omelettes).

Monterosso al mare is famous for its rice pie with dried mushrooms. On this section of the coast, seafood is abundant and anchovies are particularly prevalent on menus. Our journey then turned inland to the Tuscan landscape around Villa Branca, just outside of Florence.

Five lands

Monterosso al Mare
Vernazza
Corniglia
Manarola
Riomaggiore

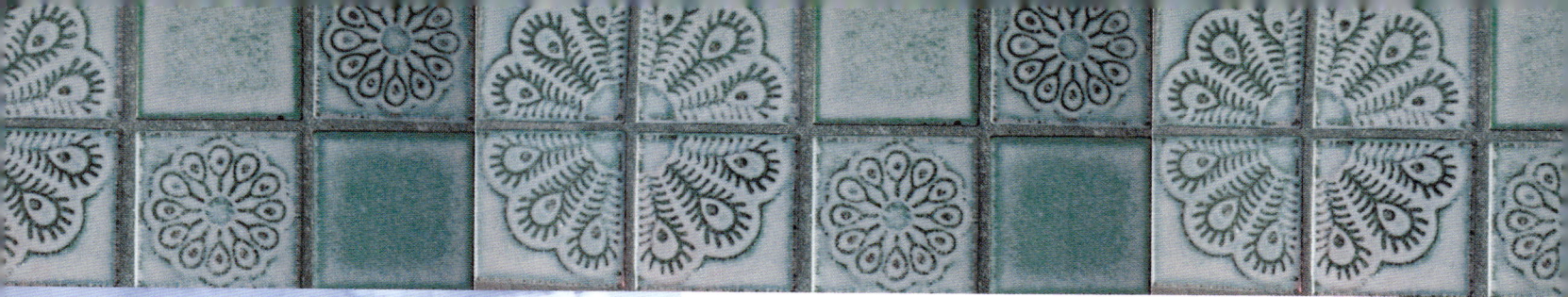

Villa & Branca

Villa Branca was the perfect location for me to host a writers' retreat for seven students. The landscape around the villa is stunning in true Tuscan style. Trees line the undulating hills, ranging from palest amber to rich honey or vivid rust. Medieval villages, villas, castles and renovated farmhouses nestle among the groves, indicative of the wealth of the families who occupied this region in Renaissance times.

On our way to Sorrento last year we had discovered Villa Branca and stopped for an elegant morning tea hosted by Robyn Vulinovich, the Villa's Australian representative.

Villa Branca is set in the heart of the Chianti Classico wine-growing district amid centuries-old oak and pine forests and dark green cypress trees which punctuate the misty olive groves and rows of vineyards.

The estate comprises the main villa and several ancient stone farmhouses, surrounded by aromatic herb gardens, lavender and wildflowers on about 150 hectares that the family, particularly the Contessa Ilaria Branca, have built into a successful wine and olive oil company. Villa Branca wines are enjoyed worldwide and Fernet Branca is one of my favourite aperitifs.

With style and rustic ambience, it was the kind of place I've always dreamed of staying, and I fell in love with it at once. I was excited that this time I could spend time soaking up the Tuscan atmosphere.

We arrived mid-morning to collect Robyn and drove to Florence to pick up my seven students for seven days of creativity in Tuscany.

Florence

We had arranged to meet the students in Florence (Firenze) at a less than classical but, we thought, easily recognisable place—McDonald's at Stazione di Santa Maria Novella.

We dropped Robyn off at the station to collect the group and waited for her return. She came back minutes later with a double whammy of bad news: firstly, Clare Clarke had all her luggage stolen from the train even before it had left Milan, and secondly there were two McDonald's at the station so our bewildered group was divided between them! Robyn and Bill rounded them up in true sheepdog fashion and, after loading them into the hired van, Florence, one of the most enchanting cities in the world, beckoned. We were all in exceptionally high spirits, including poor Clare who was left with only what she wore. We headed first to Piazzale Michelangelo for a view of the splendid city itself.

It really doesn't matter where your meandering takes you, because in this city of artists, architects and sculpture, beauty dazzles from every corner. Dante, Michelangelo, Donatello, Botticelli and Brunelleschi are just a few of the masters to have practised their art in Florence. There's so much to see that it's easy to suffer Renaissance overload, but no matter how many times we visit, Bill and I are always drawn to the world's fourth-largest cathedral, the Cattedrale di Santa Maria del Fiore. With its pink, green and white marble façade, it took 150 years to build and is one of the world's most beautiful buildings. The Baptistry, too, is breathtaking.

When you feel you just can't do justice to any more mosaics, frescoes or cathedrals, it's time to find a bar, order a glass of Chianti Classico and soak up the ambience of this captivating city. We wandered all day before setting out late afternoon for Villa Branca.

Things to see

- Immerse yourself in the artistic splendour of the Uffizi, Galleria dell'Accademia (where you can see Michelangelo's *David*) and Bargello galleries.
- Marvel at the architecture of the Duomo, Basilica di San Lorenzo, Basilica di Santa Maria Novella, and the city's oldest bridge, Ponte Vecchio.
- Discover the city's history and culture at the Museo Archeologico.

There would be time for more exploration of Florence later in the week and it is a city best enjoyed in elegant 'sips' rather than 'gulps.'

My huddle of writers was an eclectic group of six women and one young man. David Tieck was a full-time writer fresh from running a marathon in Budapest. Louise Brazenor, author of *How to be a Professional Housewife*, was a vigneron who ran a B&B in Australia. Pam Bradley, a historian, has written six books, the most recent being *Cities of Vesuvius*, and was working on her memoirs. Vicki Ponsford spoke fluent Italian and was also writing memoirs based on her work with refugees. Nerida Melville-Smith was a social worker and short story writer whose poetry had just been included in an anthology. Claire Darby loved books and aspired to own a bookshop, and Clare Clarke had little desire to write but wanted to visit Italy with a group of fun-loving, like minded people.

Despite being such a varied group, we all got along famously and quickly bonded over our shared loves of Italy and literature, so there was lots of chatter and much anticipation of great things to come as we poured into Torrione, our nine-bed villa.

First things first in Italy: food! We were all anxious to get to the *supermercato* to stock up for the week ahead.

Vicki Ponsford, a devotee of 'slow food', a move-ment dedicated to the enjoyment of eating food that has been lovingly prepared, volunteered to cook. Vicki was a long-time Italophile who started studying Italian thirty years ago and first visited in 1978. In 1980 she returned to study language and culture at the University of Florence. In 2002 she attended cooking courses at the prestigious Scuola della Cucina Italiana in Milan, so we voted her in as chef for the week and promised we would peel, chop, slice, grate, wash up and constantly top up her wine glass.

Our beautifully prepared and presented dinners were something we all looked forward to on the nights we ate at the villa, so I asked Vicki to give me some of her recipes and share her knowledge of Italian food, much of which has come from over thirty years of eating with Italian friends, tasting regional specialities and collecting local recipes.

I asked her to write a food diary of our time at Villa Branca; this is what she sent:

It was such a great adventure to cook for the group and it was fortunate that so many of us were interested in, and enjoyed, good food and wine. On the way to Villa Branca we stopped in Mercatale, the nearest village, to buy supplies for the week. Italian supermarkets have an excellent range of goods and generally stock excellent quality produce. Most also have an extensive cellar.

I bought some green and black olives, soft white cheese, pane toscano, tinned tomatoes (pomodori pelati), garlic, red onions, lemons, fresh basil, parsley, De Cecco spaghetti, fennel, salad greens, white grapes—and white wine of course! Patsy was the first into the wine cellar and the last out, but everyone enjoyed wine and stocked up, an auspicious sign!

The Villa Branca kitchen was well equipped and decorated in Tuscan style with ceramic tiles, large wooden cupboards, deep copper sinks, a large oven and an electric grill. It was a great space to work in and had a nice atmosphere. For convivial dining, there was a rectangular table, which had an extension piece so we were able to set up places for the nine of us, using the bench in the hallway for extra seating. Our complimentary pantry basket included a bottle of Villa Branca cold pressed extra virgin olive oil and a Villa Branca Riserva, the chianti from the estate—essential ingredients for la buona cucina (good cooking)! One night I cooked the mussels in white wine with spaghetti from my good friend Giorgio Pastafiglia, an artist who now works as a chef.

Fabulous Florence

The gracious city of Florence is recognised as the cradle of the Renaissance and abounds with culture, art and history.

First founded by the Etruscans in 200 BC, it sprawls on the banks of the Arno river and by 59 BC became a Roman garrison, allowing Rome easy passage to northern Italy and Gaul.

After being controlled by numerous ruling parties, Cosimo de Medici assumed control in the fifteenth century, to be followed by his grandson Lorenzo the Magnificent in 1469, whose rule heralded the revival of art, music, poetry and culture during the Renaissance and became Florence's golden age.

Mussels in white wine
with spaghetti

Serves 4–6

1 kg (2 lb) fresh mussels in their shells
1 clove of garlic
1 fresh chilli
parsley, chopped
1 tablespoon lemon rind
3 tablespoons olive oil
250 ml white wine
500 g spaghetti

Wash the mussels under running water and scrub the shells until smooth and clean. Chop garlic, chilli, parsley and lemon rind and mix together.

Heat oil in a saucepan and fry herbs for a few minutes at moderate heat. Pour in white wine, then add cleaned mussels. Place the lid on the saucepan and increase heat to steam open the shells, shaking the pan every few minutes to ensure even distribution. Check mussels and remove open shells. Replace the lid until all of the remaining shells open. Remove the mussels, take some out of their shells and discard empty shells and shells that do not open.

Cook the spaghetti in boiling salted water until al dente. Drain and place in a large serving bowl, retaining a small amount of the water. Tip steamed mussels and those still in their shells into the pasta with all juices and stir well. Add more water if necessary. Sprinkle with chopped parsley and serve.

Note: This dish goes particularly well with a glass of chilled Frascati.

Wonderful wines

Villa Branca was not only the perfect place to host a writer's retreat, it is also a working vineyard with a prestigious reputation. The estate comprises over 150 hectares, of which 55 are devoted to viticulture and the rest to olive groves. We were all looking forward to being taken on a tour of the vineyards and the fourteenth century cellars during our stay. Villa Branca produces about 120 000 bottles of wine annually, using mainly the Sangiovese grape.

Contessa Ilaria Branca has been enthusiastic about the adoption of new techniques, and production will soon increase when the re-planted vineyards come into fruit. The cellars have also recently been expanded to accommodate more ageing wines. They also produce a small amount of Vin Santo, a lovely dessert wine.

Wine is as old as the civilised world, with indications that it was produced as early as 6000 BC in Mesopotamia. It soon became important for use in rituals and religion and ancient Rome enjoyed a festival that celebrated Bacchus, the god of wine. At one time, only men were permitted to drink wine, as it was felt that women would commit adultery if they tried it and shouldn't be allowed anywhere near it! Thank goodness that idea went by the wayside!

Ancient Romans preferred their wine sweet over dry and mixed it with water. They also experimented with new flavours, including garlic, rose petals and pepper!

Italy's temperate climate and soil are excellent for wine production and Italians are justifiably proud of their wines.

Laws control wine clarification and quality. If wine has DOC (Controlled Denomination of Origin) and DOCG (Controlled and Guaranteed Denomination of Origin) they represent superior quality for their area and grape type. VDT classifications are for *vino da tavola*—table wines, and give no indication of area, wine type or year and are at the bottom of the scale. Indicated Geographic Specifications (IGT) are mid-range.

The price of wine is determined by classification but we have no complaints about the table wines we frequently drank. The eight northern regions produce about a third of all Italian wine, but account for more than half of the DOC/DOCG total.

Veneto produces both red and white wines. Soave comes from Verona, as does Valpolicella and Bardolino. Friuli-Venezia produces excellent white wines. Lombardy is known for its red and sparkling wines, but the most famous reds in the north are Barolo and Barbaresco from Piedmont. Orvieto in Umbria is well-known for its whites, and has two famous reds, Montefalco Sagrantino and Torgiano Rosso Riserva.

Perhaps Italy's most famous wine is Chianti from Tuscany, which can be either red or white, but the red wines Brunello di Montalcino and Vino Nobile di Montepulciano are the most popular.

Other favourites are Verdicchio dei Castelli di Jesi Classico, said to be the best wine to drink with fish, and Barbera, a robust red.

Rome is best known for its white wines—Frascati (which goes well with fish and chicken), Marino, Castelli Romani and the famous Est! Est! Est!

Many delis and butcher shops allow you to pay 10 euro for a ticket that can be used to sample wines over a few days. You choose the wine from a flask labelled with the wine and the cost per tasting—around 2 euro for a cheaper wine and 5 euro for a better quality wine. We were lucky enough to enjoy a wine tasting at Villa Branca, where we could draw on the expertise of Dr Markus Holzinger (opposite) who guided us through wine after wine in the enormous cellar.

Snapper fillets
with white wine & parsley

Serves 4

½ cup (2 oz) plain flour
1 teaspoon coarse ground pepper
¼ teaspoon sea salt
4 x 220 g (7 oz) snapper fillets
2 tablespoons olive oil

60 g (2 oz) butter
2 cloves garlic, crushed
½ cup (4 fl oz) white wine
2 tablespoons fresh parsley, finely chopped

Combine flour, pepper and salt in a dish and coat fish fillets evenly with flour, shaking off excess. Heat oil in a pan, add fish, and cook over a medium heat for 5–6 minutes on each side, depending on thickness of fish. Set fish aside on a serving plate and keep warm.

Wipe out the pan, then melt butter, add garlic, and cook for 2 minutes. Add white wine and simmer until sauce reduces. Just before serving, add parsley to the sauce and serve over fish.

Meat

Nobody on our retreat was a vegetarian, and we were all definitely canivores (*carne* means meat). We'd heard about Dario Cecchini of Panzano (who is known as the poet butcher and is the most famous butcher in Tuscany) and couldn't wait to meet him. Panzano is a quaint hilltop village located only 3 kilometres from Villa Branca, 35 km from Florence and Siena, on the 222 Highway, known affectionately as the *strada di vino*.

At 10 am on Sunday, market day, this 'village of gourmands' was alive with stalls of every kind manned by local growers who set up imaginative arrangements of fruit, fish, novelty hardware, shoes, clothes, handbags, scarves and colourful tablecloths.

As we wandered up the narrow street to Dario's *macelleria*, which has been running for 250 years, people were already spilling out onto the street munching homemade Tuscan sausage and drinking red wine. Outside a young man sat on a rickety chair, strumming a guitar and singing softly to himself.

It was a most unusual butcher shop! Inside the tiny shop, classical music and the aroma of fresh herbs and spices filled the air while customers pressed against the glass showcases where meats of all kinds were displayed.

A young man thrust a glass of red wine into my hands while another chopped Cosimino, a large meat-loaf named after Cosimo de Medici. Another passed me some lard on bread (which tastes better than it sounds). Bill munched happily on bruschetta with tomatoes and olives—everyone was shouting over the din of conversations in German, French and Spanish.

Dario laughed and joked with his regular customers, who lined up two and three deep as he carved chunks of cooked meat off huge carcasses and wrapped them in cones of white paper. I found myself pinned against the tiled wall, where prosciuttos were ageing. It was like being at a party—a wild party!

Within minutes we were toasting everyone we could think of—the Mayor of Panzano, the President of Italy and Sophia Loren—while we ate porchetta and spicy sausage.

Another interesting butcher shop we visited was the Antica Macelleria Falorni in Greve. From every centimetre of the ceiling hung carcasses of different animals. Outside the shop is a stuffed wild boar, *cinghiale,* which are abundant in the wild. There was wild boar salami, Tuscan capocollo salami made from the pig's head and neck, Siena salami flavoured with garlic and wild fennel, huge slabs of rigatino steso, Tuscan bacon cured for four months on aromatic wooden boards and with just the thinnest layer of fat.

Polpettone

Serves 4–6

2 slices white bread, crusts removed
¼ cup (2 fl oz) milk
500 g (1 lb) pork mince
2 rashers rindless bacon, diced
2 cloves of garlic, crushed
1 egg
¼ teaspoon ground nutmeg
1 teaspoon dried marjoram
2 hard-boiled eggs
3 chipolatas

Preheat oven to 180°C (350°F/Gas Mark 4).
Soak bread in milk for 5 minutes.

Place mince, bacon, garlic, egg, nutmeg, marjoram and bread in a bowl. Mix well with your fingertips. Press mixture, on a lightly floured surface, into a 10 x 20 cm (4 x 8 in) rectangle. Slice eggs in half and place with chipolatas along the centre of the meat. Roll meat around filling. Place in a greased roasting pan and bake for 1 hour or until cooked. Serve hot.

Arrosto Fiorentino

Dario Cecchini's famous Beef Florentine recipe.

1 kg (2lb) of beef suitable for roasting
½ cup fresh rosemary leaves
1 cup fresh sage
125 ml (4 fl oz) extra virgin olive oil
salt
fresh chilli pepper

Let the meat come to room temperature and preheat the oven to 230°C/450°F (Gas Mark 8).

Prepare an infusion by finely chopping the rosemary, sage and chilli. Place in a small bowl and cover with olive oil. Sprinkle with salt and whisk until blended.

Place the beef in a shallow roasting pan and cook uncovered for 35 minutes. Remove from the oven and pour the herb infusion over the beef. Cover with foil and leave to sit for 10 minutes until ready to serve. Slice the beef thinly and serve with herb infused oil. This makes a great buffet dish served at room temperature.

Next to it hung guanciale gota, a type of streaky bacon made from pig's cheek and used since ancient times as an economical flavouring. It has only recently been discovered by lovers of fine cuisine and is ideal for seasoning any kind of roast meat and as an essential ingredient in Pasta All'amatriciana and pasta Carbonara.

I tasted the salami piccante puro suino, which is a delicious hot salami of pure pork spiced with chilli peppers and paprika. Finocchiona Briciolona, obtained from fat and lean meats from pork belly, has a rather velvety taste. It is crumbly in texture and is flavoured with wild fennel and sprinkled with the local Greve wine and is absolutely delicious—different from anything I've ever eaten.

Finally, I squeezed in a slice of the Tuscan home-style ham, which is eaten with a chunk of unsalted bread. And all this before dinner! The butcher had thoughtfully, and amusingly, produced a little brochure instructing customers how to take care of his salami. It read:

When you are taking home your salami you should be making sure not to expose him to sun and try not to crush him. It is important for his happiness to keep him in a comfortable place, cool, so he can keep continuing his slow perspiration. When this has started to be happening, please then you can put him in the refrigerator and be putting some paper over the cut surfaces to keep in his moisture. Then he will stay with his flavours.

It struck me that, aside from the cut surfaces and refrigeration part, this could apply to some of the men I had known in the past!

Dario's mad cow

When mad cow disease swept through Europe and Italy in the 1980s and the sale of beef was banned, Dario Cecchini, the Meat Maestro, arranged a funeral lamenting the death of the beef industry and with it one of his Florentine specialties, Arrosto Fiorentino. Television cameras whirred as his grand memorial parade, complete with bands, pomp and ceremony befitting an important funeral, took place outside his shop. During the mad cow crisis, he kept a rose underneath the cow's head (left) outside his shop.

Char-grilled lamb with
mint pesto & creamy potatoes

Serves 4–6

4 lamb backstraps (500 g/1 lb each)
salt and freshly ground black pepper

Creamy potatoes
500 g (1 lb) potatoes, thinly sliced
salt and freshly ground black pepper
1 teaspoon nutmeg slices
1 tablespoon plain (all-purpose) flour
1 garlic clove, crushed
40 g (1⅓ oz) parmesan cheese, grated
1 cup (8 fl oz) 250ml fresh cream

Mint pesto
1 cup (2 oz) fresh mint leaves
½ cup (1 oz) fresh parsley leaves
2 cloves of garlic
½ cup (3 oz) pine nuts, toasted
3 tablespoons pecorino cheese, grated
⅓ cup (2¾ fl oz) olive oil
salt and freshly ground black pepper

Preheat oven to 180°C (350°F/Gas Mark 4). Season lamb with salt and freshly ground pepper and set aside.

Grease an ovenproof dish with butter and arrange potato in overlapping rows in the dish, seasoning between each layer with salt, pepper, garlic and nutmeg. Mix flour, parmesan cheese and cream and pour over potatoes. Sprinkle with extra parmesan then bake in the oven for 40–45 minutes or until cooked.

To make the mint pesto place 3 tablespoons grated parmesan cheese, grated mint, parsley, garlic, pine nuts and cheese in the bowl of a food processor and process until finely chopped. Add olive oil in a steady stream with the processor still running. Season with salt and pepper to taste then set aside.

Preheat barbecue plate (or pan), and grease lightly with a little oil. Char-grill the lamb on both sides for approximately 5–10 minutes or until done to your liking.

Serve lamb, sliced diagonally, on a bed of the creamy potatoes with the mint pesto on top.

Celebrations

Robyn suggested the ristorante Oltre Il Giardino for lunch, where we shared a mushroom and wild boar risotto, which the chef explained took two days to prepare as the boar is marinated slowly in wine and herbs. Talk about slow food! After a glass (or two) of a Santa Margherita Pinot Grigio from Orvieto, we set out for the medieval hilltop village is of Monteriggioni.

Monteriggioni has been famous since the Middle Ages, so famous that the poet Dante Alighieri referred to it in the *Divine Comedy*. Dante was apparently in the town during one of its great battles which spurred him to write the famous simile of giants chained around Malebolge. The village a walled town that dates back to the thirteenth century, when it was built in just six years around a pre-existing fortified farm of Lombard origins for use as a garrison town.

Monteriggioni is without doubt testament to a bygone era, and one of the most amazing and memorable towns we've ever visited. The town is encircled by high walls containing fourteen heavily fortified towers which were constructed to guard against the Florentine invasion.

The perfectly preserved walls are an amazing feat of engineering, covering over 500 metres and stretching between the towers and two gates. We went to the piazza in what is normally a sleepy little town of 44 residents and were thrilled to find the annual feast of the Assumption of the Madonna was in full swing.

The piazza was packed with villagers in suits of armour, long velvet pantaloons and wonderful feathered hats. Young and old alike wore medieval costume and walked slowly in procession behind the priest, who bore aloft a huge crucifix.

The sombre procession wound slowly through the cobble stoned streets to the church, where the priest held high a magnificent painting of the Madonna Assunta that had been brought from the museum in Siena for the festival.

The villagers all took their roles very seriously, but when they returned to the piazza, the mood became more relaxed. We stood in front of the pretty Romanesque church and watched the band, resplendent in their bright blue jackets. Next came the girls' band, with batons twirling and skirts swirling, and we joined in singing and clapping.

On returning to Villa Branca we shared a few bottles of wine and our last meal with the students.

Fair Verona

Our next stop was the World Heritage city of Verona, one of the prettiest and most prosperous towns in the north. Looming over the town is the impressive Castelvecchio, built in 1375 and now home to the Museo Civico d'Arte, which showcases a collection of medieval and Renaissance art, swords, shields, suits of armour and ancient jewellery. Bill and I strolled through the castle and over the Ponte Scaligero bridge, which leads over the Adige river.

Verona is home to the greatest number of Roman ruins after Rome itself, and the huge first-century AD Arena, off the bustling and amusingly named Piazza Bra, is the third-largest amphitheatre in the world and draws many visitors. It is remarkably well-preserved and is still used as an operatic concert venue today.

As the arena is generally less crowded than the Colosseum, when you walk through the underground passages or sit on the marble seats, which could fit nearly the entire population of the city in AD 30, you get a real sense of what it must have felt like to have been there on a performance day, hearing the roar of the crowd as the gladiators and exotic beasts met their unfortunate fates.

Of course, being a literature lover, the real cause of my visit to Verona was the chance to see Juliet's Balcony at the Casa di Giulietta, where I had visions of Bill swooning up at me from below while I gazed romantically heavenwards. But Bill did manage to capture a lovely picture of the balcony while I gazed misty eyed at the fluttering love letters, engagement proposals and 'Shane loves Sheree' post-it notes plastered to the walls of the enclosure by star-crossed lovers from around the world.

I nudged Bill. 'Isn't it romantic, darling?' I whispered, digging in my purse for a post-it note. Bill inspected the wall for a moment and then said, most ungallantly I thought, 'It's unhygenic that's what it is. Look at that, they're all stuck on with chewing gum!'

The jury is still out on whether the Capulet family ever inhabited that house, but what is certain is that Shakespeare used poetic licence to tell a tale recorded by Luigi da Porto in the 1520s of the 'Two households, both alike in dignity, in fair Verona.'

After snacking on pizza, we strolled the busy streets, pausing to admire handicrafts at the colourful markets in Piazza Erbe, which was a Roman Forum in ancient times. The square is dominated by the Baroque Palazzo Mafei, built in 1668, and to its east is the Casa dei Mercanti.

The province of Veneto is known for its many colourful carnivals, most often involving masks. Verona celebrates an annual gastronomic festival, the

Two ho... Two households both a like in dignity in F... Verona
in Fair i... in Fair Verona
Two ho... Two hous...

Two households, both a like in dignity in Fair Verona
dignity in Fair Verona Two households, both a like in digni...
Two households, both a like in dignity in Fair Verona

Things to see

- Visit the Teatro Romano on the opposite side of the Adige River, or learn more about Veronese history at the nearby Museo Archaelogico.
- Pretend you are an opera singer at the Arena.
- The Duomo, Verona's beautiful Romanesque cathedral has been standing since 1139.
- Step back to medieval days at Castelvecchio.
- Visit the church of San Zeno, the most ornate Romanesque church in northern Italy.
- See Juliet's house and Romeo's house nearby.

Baccanale del Gnoc or *Venerdi Grasso*, which literally translates as Fat Friday. The carnival has its origins in the sixteenth century when, during famine, the price of flour skyrocketed so high that the bakers refused to make bread. Wealthy citizens, including Dr Tammaso Da Vico, now considered the father of carnevale, gave the starving people of the San Zeno quarter free flour, cheese and wine. Nowadays, a king of the carnevale (*Papa del Gnocco*) is elected and must wear a big fake belly full of gnocchi and carry a fork as a sceptre. Every district of the city has its own mask and each has a float in the large procession, after which gnocchi di san Zeno is distributed to the crowd. The gnocchi sauce is melted butter and cheese, but the traditional sauce is based on another famine-fighting Veronese dish: pastissada de caval.

Legend has it that King Theodoric of the Ostogoths fought a particularly prolonged and bloody battle with a nearby king around Verona. Wanting to share his triumph with the (yet again) starving Veronese, he let the people eat the flesh of any horses killed on the battlefield. After the long and brutal battle, the meat

was less than fresh, so, to mask the smell, the townsfolk marinated it with onions, and lots of wine—to great success obviously as pastissada de caval is still eaten today.

By far my favourite tale of Verona's bizarre culinary past is that of peara sauce, first sampled by the unfortunate Dona Lombarda. During a banquet, Dona's husband forced her to drink out of the skull of her assassinated father, causing her, rather understandably, to lose her appetite for some time. Many chefs tried to tempt her tastebuds with their creations, but it was a peara sauce that made her regain her appetite—and her strength, upon which she very wisely had her husband assassinated.

History

Verona was ruled by the Scaligeri family from 1263 before falling to the Viconti of Milin in 1387. Later, Venice, France, and Verona ruled in succession until 1866.

Peara sauce

Peara Sauce is traditionally served over boiled meats, but can be used as a kind of gravy for most meats.

Serves 6–8

2 tablespoons butter
2 cups dry breadcrumbs
4–5 cups of meat broth or stock
2 tablespoons of ground parmesan
salt and pepper to taste

Mealt the butter and add the breadcrumbs to soak up the butter. Pour in the broth and add a pinch of salt. The consistency should be thick and creamy, not too soup-like.
Reduce the heat to a gentle simmer and cover, letting it simmer for 3 hours and stirring occasionally. After three hours, check the saltiness and add a little more salt if necessary.
Just before serving add the parmesan and pepper.
The peppery flavour should be apparent but shouldn't overwhelm the tastebuds.

Cinnamon zabaglione

Serves 4

This scrumptious Italian dessert is another Yves Pagni speciality!

130 g sugar
4 egg yolks
100 ml white wine
100 ml of sweet wine

Place the yolks, sugar and wine in a small saucepan. Normally, zabaglione is placed in a bain marie and whipped until set, but the preparation this way can take up to 15 minutes. I recommend cooking it in the saucepan at a low heat and whipping, without stopping, until the right thickness is achieved. This will usually take only about 3–4 minutes. Don't let it come to the boil.
As soon as it's ready, serve it in bowls and dust the top lightly with ground cinnamon.

Venice

If you think Verona is romantic, then the logical step on any trip to northern Italy has to be Venice, arguably the most romantic city in the world, but definitely the most romantic sinking city in the world!

Venice (Venezia) is situated on a series of low banks lapped by the waters of the Adriatic Sea, which in the autumn sometimes spills into the Piazza San Marco and pools into a glimmering lake at the foot of St Mark's Basilica.

This unique city built around a Grand Canal and a series of smaller lagoons and waterways first sprang up in the fifth and sixth centuries. Mainland Italians fled to the almost uninhabitable coast to escape barbarian Hun invasions after the decline of the Roman Empire. They fashioned rafts and connected them with wooden walkways, then went right ahead and built grand buildings, houses and palaces on top of them!

Venice's unusual location demands an equally innovative form of transport—the colourful curved-hulled gondola, which has been the traditional form of transport since the eleventh century. Also plying the busy, watery 'streets' of Venice are the much cheaper *traghetti*, gondola ferries that take you just across the other side of the grand canal, and larger commercial waterbuses (*vaporetti*). Venice is home to some of the most recognisable sights in the world—the Rialto Bridge, St Mark's, the Bridge of Sighs and the Doge's Palace.

The richly ornamental Roman Catholic St Mark's Basilica on Piazza San Marco, the only Piazza in Venice, comes with its own slightly morbid history. In the year 828 AD two Venetian merchants visiting Alexandria in Egypt made off with the body of the apostle Saint Mark the Evangelist. They brought his body, a religious relic, to Venice where it was at first installed in the Doge's Palace while a grand new place of worship was built, modelled on the Church of the Twelve Apostles in Constantinople and consecrated in 1094.

You can still see the shrine housing poor St Mark's shin bones today, but Bill and I were more astounded by the lavishly spectacular interior, where golden mosaics gleam from the domed ceilings, walls and floors, framing the jewel-encrusted altarpiece of the Pala d'Oro with its 250 enamel religious paintings.

The treasury hoards silver, gold and precious jewels. It truly reflects Venice's historic position as the jewel of the Adriatic—a flourishing and affluent maritime city that controlled much of Europe's sea trade.

Today, Venice's canal side markets throng with tourists and ring to the sounds of vendors spruiking

Bridge of Sighs

The Bridge of Sighs, or Ponte dei Sospiri, has rather a romantic reputation, but the name only really became popular in the nineteenth century when used by the poet Lord Byron. The bridge's actual purpose is hardly romantic. The white limestone bridge connects the interrogation rooms of the Doge's Palace with the prison, causing prisoners crossing it to sigh at their last glimpse of Venice and freedom.

against the splash of oars striking the waves, but early in the eleventh century Venice became the gateway to Byzantium.

Exotic spices such as cinnamon and cardamon, vividly dyed fabrics, relics from Constantinople and much sought after coffee were all available in Venice, which by the seventeenth century had become renowned for its decadence as much as its extravagance.

Gambling was a popular pastime of the nobility, who lolled in coffee shops in their elaborate, powdered wigs and hinted at their sexual proclivities and preferences with carefully placed beauty spots called *moshe*. It must have been very frustrating indeed if you just happened to have a freckle in a place that meant something you didn't want to say!

Around about this time, Giacomo Casanova became the first of many legendary Venetian suitors ending up in the prison accessed by the Bridge of Sighs, but eventually escaping to continue philandering for many a year in Paris.

We visited the Rialto Bridge and wandered through the many small squares the Venetians call *campi*. We were lucky enough to see the most gorgeous wedding, complete with cherubic page-boys dressed in frilled lace shirts and a beautiful sun-kissed bride escorted by her wedding guests.

Markets and boutique stores caught our attention, as did the many dramatic masks that hung in most shop windows and dangled from the colourful umbrellas above market stalls. The masks are for sale all year round but are primarily for the Carnevale, when the streets are filled with revellers dressed in eighteenth-century masquerade costumes. The use of theatrical masks in Venice dates back to the thirteenth century

Things to see

- Take a gondola ride under the Rialto Bridge, built by Antonio da Ponte in 1591.
- Visit the Accademia gallery, home to five centuries of paintings, from Byzantine to Baroque.
- The Doge's Palace (Palazzo Ducale) is a ninth-century gothic masterpiece and was the residence of all of Venice's rulers.

when it gave wealthy nobles the chance to engage in licentious behaviour with anonymous members of the lower class.

Once the Venetian republic fell in the eighteenth century, promiscuity was frowned upon and the use of masks fell out of favour and disappeared.

The extravagant Carnevale was reintroduced in 1979 and has been the highlight of the Venetian calendar ever since. Swarms of tourists, celebrities and paparazzi desend on Venice during Carnevale and bring the streets and canals to life with their colourful costumes, wigs and masks. Much as I would have enjoyed the spectacle,

Bill and I visited at a less crowded time. After taking in the delights during the day, we were footsore and hungry by the time we began hunting for a Venetian restaurant. Unlike most places in Italy, the Venetians eat early. You'll be lucky to find a restaurant after 9.30 pm!

Venetian cooking is dominated by rice dishes, like the famous *risi e bisi*, beans, polenta and seafood, but has retained an eastern influence acquired from its heyday as a trade centre. Radicchio is used in many ways and commonly added to risotto, while sardelle in saor (sweet and sour sardines) is a traditional dish that has changed little since the 1300s.

Fish 10

Italy is surrounded by sea and blessed with many large lakes and rivers full of fish (*pesce*), so it is not surprising that the cuisine incorporates some excellent seafood dishes.

Near the coast, tuna (*tonno*), monkfish (*coda di rospo*), swordfish (*pesce spada*), sole (*sogliola*) and red mullet (*triglia*) abound and are used, with shellfish and octopus, to make hearty stews and *frutti di mare*.

Anchovies (*acciughe*) and sardines (*sarde*) are plentiful and are found in many dishes, especially in Verona and Venice on Italy's north-eastern coast, although they are also prevalent in the south.

Bill and I found that most regions have a version of a popular dish called *baccala*, a kind of dried, salted codfish. Freshwater fish, such as trout (*trota*), carp (*carpione*) and perch (*pesce persico*) are common on menus inland, where they are mostly offered baked whole with olive oil, lemon juice and herbs, or grilled, rather than in mixed concoctions.

In coastal villages, seafood can be purchased daily and the cornucopia of delights includes prawns (*gamberetti*), clams (*vongole*), mussels (*cozze*) and octopus (*polpi*) as well as its squid cousin (*calamari*).

Fish chowders and seafood soups are also popular.

Sardine fritters
with minted chilli butter

Serves 4

12 fresh sardine fillets
4 tablespoons plain flour
1 egg, blended with 2 tablespoons milk
125 g (4 oz) dried breadcrumbs
oil for cooking

Minted chilli butter
125 g (4 oz) butter, softened
3 tablespoons fresh mint, finely chopped
2 spring onions, finely chopped
1 clove garlic, crushed
¼ teaspoon red chilli, chopped
freshly ground black pepper to taste

To make minted chilli butter, place butter, mint, spring onions, garlic, chilli and pepper in a bowl and mix well. Place butter mixture on a piece of plastic clingwrap and roll into a log shape. Refrigerate until required.

Coat sardines in flour, dip in egg then coat with breadcrumbs.

Heat oil and one-third of the minted chilli butter in a large frying pan and cook sardines for 1–2 minutes each side or until golden. Serve sardines topped with a curl of minted chilli butter.

Seafood tagliatelle

Serves 4

400 g (13 oz) tagliatelle
1 cup (8 fl oz) chicken stock
500 g (1 lb) washed marinara mix (mussels, fish, prawns/shrimps, oysters, calamari/squid)
25 g (1 oz) butter
1 finely chopped onion
3 tablespoons plain (all-purpose) flour
250 g (8 oz) carton light sour cream
2 tablespoons of chopped fresh parsley

Cook pasta in boiling salted water for 15 minutes or until al dente. Drain well.

Heat stock in deep frying pan and poach marinara mix until cooked. Drain, reserving the liquid.

Melt butter in a saucepan and sauté onion for 5 minutes or until translucent. Stir in flour and cook until frothy. Pour in fish liquid and cook, stirring until sauce boils and thickens. Stir in sour cream, parsley and marinara mix. Bring to boiling point, but do not boil. Pour over cooked pasta and serve.

Spicy prawns
with sun-dried tomatoes

Serves 4

3 tablespoons olive oil
1 kg (2 lb) green king prawns peeled, de-veined, tails intact
1 tablespoon tomato paste
2 teaspoons brown sugar
2 cloves garlic, crushed
1 tablespoon chilli sauce
1 tablespoon fresh coriander (cilantro)
¾ cup (6 oz) sun-dried tomatoes
1 tablespoon fresh lime juice
snow pea sprouts (mange-tout sprouts)

Heat oil in a frying pan over moderate heat. Add prawns and cook for 1 minute each side. Remove prawns with a slotted spoon and set aside. Add tomato paste, sugar, garlic, chilli sauce and coriander to frying pan and cook for 1 minute.

Return prawns to frying pan, add drained sun-dried tomatoes, toss in chilli sauce and sprinkle with lime juice. Place prawns on a serving dish. Garnish with snow pea sprouts and serve.

Naples

We headed south to Naples, a major seaport and the third largest city in Italy. Napoli sprawls around the edge of the spectacular Bay of Naples. For many years it has dominated the south, the Mezzo-giorno, land of the midday sun. The city is perfectly positioned as a starting place for visits to Vesuvius, Pompeii and Herculaneum, as well as the pretty islands of Capri, Procida, Ischia and Sicily. We found it one of the most tumultuous, vibrant and exciting cities in Italy.

Naples was established by the Greeks and later, under Roman rule, became a favourite haunt for Pompey, Tiberius and Caesar. Despite waves of invasions by the Goths, Normans, Hohenstaufens, French and Spanish, Naples flourished. Much of its artistic and architectural splendour comes from this later period as the Italians absorbed cultures from their captors.

Today, there is a juxtaposition of great wealth, from shipyards, porcelain, petroleum and steel industries, with poverty and unemployment. But the staunchly Catholic inhabitants are proud of their traditions and there is a robustness reflected in Neopolitan joviality, music and food.

The Neopolitans' laughter and delight in eating and drinking makes this city a wonderful place to visit. There are never as many tourists in Naples as we encounter in other Italian cities and towns, but the bars and ristoranti teem with noisy locals, who shout regularly in their ebullient dialect.

Neapolitans love to sing, loudly. There were many nights in Naples when our quiet dinner developed into karaoke-style renditions of Neapolitan songs with a piano accordionist and dancing—with the other diners, if not the waiters! In our search for a pretty bar to relax in after the drive, and enjoy a Campari soda, we ducked and dodged as mopeds buzzed by and cars and scooters, horns tooting, wove in and out of the traffic—and one another. Although we were in an *area pedonale* (supposedly the safe zone for pedestrians!) a moped suddenly leap-frogged the kerb slicing between us, the driver waving and grinning broadly as he checkily squeesed his way back in at the top of the traffic jam!

No one stops to give way and not only are traffic lights ignored—to my astonishment—but so are one-way signs! Neapolitans don't like rules and regulations—I'm always amused to see people sitting right under a *non fumare* sign, smoking without a care in the world.

Naples is noisy with traffic, shouting, music and horns, but it's this very pulsating that makes it what it is—a crazy, chaotic city that mustn't be missed.

Song & dance

Whenever Bill and I think of Italy it's hard not to think of merriment and music. Renowned for the composers Verdi, Puccini, Bellini, Donizetti and Rossini, Italy's musical history includes a sixteenth-century Venetian who printed the first musical scores with movable type. The system of musical notation is an Italian invention, as is the piano and the famous Stradivarius violin.

Italians love to sing, and their famous operatic stars include Luciano Pavarotti, who sang with the Three Tenors' first concert in Rome. Modern music owes much to Italian-American crooners like Enzo Caruso, Mario Lanza and Frank Sinatra.

The most famous folk dance is the lively tarantella, which grew out of hysteria prevalent in the city of Taranto in the fifteenth century, when it was thought that frenzied dancing would cure the bite of the Tarantula. Today's dancing often shows the same wild abandon.

Finiculi Finicula

The Finiculi Finicula song originates from the Isle of Capri off the coast of Sorrento. In the early 1950s the Italian Government built a tram that climbed the hill to the city of Capri for passengers and supplies. But everyone was too afraid to ride on it. The local government hired an advertising company to promote the use of the tram. After trying and failing with many approaches they commissioned a song—Finiculi Finicula—that became world famous. The experiment was successful and today the tram is used by everyone.

Stasera, nian mia, viam sul' monte
Un passo c'e. Un passo c'e.
Si vede Francia, Portceddu, la Spagna, lo vbegoo a te. lo vegga a te.
La testa gira gira intorno intorno
Intorno a te. Intorno a te.
E il cuore canta come il primo giorno.
Ti sposa a me. Ti sposa a me.
Lesti, lesti via'l monton' su lu
Lesti, lesti via'l monton' su la
Finiculi, finicula, finiculi fincula
Via'l monton su la, finiculi finicula.

Pasta

The origins of pasta have been much debated, with many people debunking the idea that Marco Polo brought pasta to Italy from China. But with the recent discovery of prehistoric 4000-year-old noodles in China, it is possible to say with some certainty that Italy's most famous export was an introduced delicacy. It became so integral to the Italian diet that in the thirteenth century the Pope set standards of quality for pasta.

Not that it really matters because pasta, like the tomato and pizza, is now synonymous with Italian cuisine. Today it is eaten throughout the world and in over 600 different shapes with a multitude of different sauces and seasonings.

Traditionally, pasta is made only from flour made from durum wheat, water and salt, however on the Ligurian coast, influenced by French cooking, eggs are sometimes also incorporated.

Pasta is relatively simple to make fresh and where once it was carefully rolled out by hand and cut into strips or fashioned into shapes, today machines are available to help. Its elasticity allows for a variety of uses. Thin sheets cocoon meats, cheese and vegetables to create time-honoured favourites such as ravioli, cannelloni, tortellini and cappeletti.

Thin strands make fettuccine, spaghetti, linguine and the thinnest of all *capelli d'angelo* (angel's hair), my favourite.

Bow ties, spirals, penne and shells are more creative shapes. Pasta can also be coloured with sun-dried tomato, spinach or squid ink.

Not to be overlooked is possibly the most famous type of Italian pasta—lasagne. Lasagne pays homage to almost all of the staples of Italian cuisine with its layers of meaty, tomato, garlic- and herb-flavoured filling, slathered with bechamel sauce and crowned with mozzarella.

Most Italians consider pasta, in some form, an essential part of their daily diet, and pasta dishes, flavoured with tomato, seafood or creamy sauces, prevail throughout Italy.

Pasta is usually served in portions of around 90 grams (the uncooked weight) so as not to overwhelm digestion.

To cook pasta, place small amounts in a large amount of boiling salted water and cook until it is *al dente* (to the tooth), which means that it is still a little firm when bitten.

Pork & sage ravioli

Serves 6

Pasta dough
1 tablespoon salt
3 tablespoons olive oil
5 eggs
375 g (12 oz) plain (all-purpose) flour
1 quantity Anna's Tomato Sauce (see page 162)
grated fresh parmesan cheese

Pork and sage filling
315 g (10 oz) drained ricotta cheese
60g (2 oz) finely chopped lean bacon
155g (5 oz) finely diced lean cooked pork
1 teaspoon finely chopped fresh parsley
½ teaspoon finely chopped fresh sage
1 teaspoon grated parmesan cheese
grated nutmeg and freshly ground black pepper to taste

To make the pasta dough combine salt, olive oil and eggs in a food processor. Gradually add flour, pulsing to mix. The dough is ready when it clings together and feels springy.

To make the pork and sage filling, mix ricotta cheese, bacon, pork, parsley, sage and parmesan cheese in a bowl. Season with nutmeg and black pepper. Cover and set aside while making pasta.

Divide pasta dough into quarters. Roll each quarter until it is 3 mm (⅛ in) thick, and a rectangular shape. Cut dough lengthways (use a pastry cutter) into strips 12 cm (5 in) wide.

Place 2 teaspoons of filling in the centre of one half of each strip of pastry every 8.5 cm (3½ in) then fold over the other half covering the filling. Seal the whole strip by pressing the long edges together with the prongs of a fork.

Press the two layers of pastry together between the mounds of filling and cut in the middle between mounds with the pastry cutter, again sealing the cut edges with the prongs of a fork.

Add ravioli gradually, about a third at a time, to a large saucepan of rapidly boiling, salted water. Cook for 20 minutes or until tender. Remove with a slotted spoon and drain well.

Heat the tomato sauce and serve over the ravioli. Sprinkle with parmesan cheese if desired.

Anna's tomato sauce

Makes 1 750ml bottle

2 kilos for washed, cored, ripe tomatoes
1 onion
2 tablsepoons olive oil
1 garlic clove, crushed

½ cup white wine
finely chopped fresh parsley
chopped fresh basil
salt and pepper to taste

Cut tomatoes into four wedges. Chop one onion very finely and fry in olive oil. Chop one clove of garlic very finely and add to the onion. Fry both till golden colour. Add ½ cup of white wine and simmer and bring to boil. Turn to low and cook gently for about two hours. Add salt and pepper to taste and add finely chopped fresh parsley and chopped basil.

For bottling: make double or triple quantities and put tomato mixture through a mincing machine and only cook the onions and garlic. Cook later in the bottle.

Pasta al ragu

This wonderful recipe comes from my friend Anna La Torraca and was passed down from her nonna, Gasomine Abignano who lived in the province of Avalino, just east of Naples.

Serves 4

1 small onion
2 cloves of garlic
chopped parsley
olive oil
500 g chuck steak
parmesan cheese
1 cup of red or white wine
500 g spaghetti, spirals or penne
2 kg fresh tomatoes or a bottle of Anna's homemade tomato sauce

Fry chopped onion, garlic and parsley in oil. Pound the chuck steak. Add to the pan more parsley, garlic, pepper and salt and a little freshly grated parmesan cheese. Roll up the steak and tie with a piece of string then fry in the garlic onion mixture till golden, adding 1 cup red or white wine and simmering. When the liquid is reduced by half, add tomatoes and cook for a couple of hours. Remove the string and slice the meat. Serve the meat on top of the pasta garnished with parsley and extra parmesan.

Sorrento

On the Sorrento coast, majestic grey cliffs and steep ravines rise out of the deep azure sea. It's one of the most stunning coastlines we've ever seen and with its mild year-round climate, it's not surprising that it was a favourite summer holiday destination for patricians and luminaries such as Goethe, Nietzsche, Keats, Lord Byron, Wagner and Dickens.

The history of the peninsula indicates the early presence of Phoenicians and Greeks, but it later became a Roman colony until the collapse of the Empire, when it became the Duchy of Sorrento. Much of the peninsula was seriously damaged by the eruption of Mt Vesuvius in 79 AD. The climate lends itself to growing olives and citrus trees, but also to viticulture, and, being on the coast, fish and crustaceans feature on most menus.

Bill and I happily savour the seafood of the Amalfi Coast, so by 11 am we decided to have an early lunch. We wandered down to the sea front at Marina Piccola, where the hydrofoils and ferries arrive, and were lost in reverie when a dark-skinned young waiter almost leapt on top of us.

'Come, signora, eat here, papa's place. Eat mamma's cooking. You must! Come!'

We couldn't refuse such an exuberant invitation so within minutes his papa had settled us into a table while his mamma brought over a plate of plump olives and a basket of still-warm bread. I feasted on fresh octopus and Bill had lobster, washed down with a glass each of Lacrima Christi (tears of Christ) which our young waiter told us is grown on the slopes of Vesuvius.

We're a pretty uncomplaining pair, but the hotel restaurant where we ate that night for dinner served us meat that was red raw, for me, and charcoal black, for Bill. This uncomplaining pair complained. Imagine our amusement to see a note on the dining room door the next morning:

Kindly to please not be complaining about the food. The chef is being now made very nervous.

Positively Positano

As we drove south from Sorrento towards Positano, the traffic grew heavier and slower. If you've ever been to the Amalfi Coast, you'll be breaking out in a sweat yourself with the memory of it!

The roads are narrower than any we have ever seen, barely wide enough for one car, let alone two. It would, perhaps, be possible to drive along these roads in reasonable safety if only the Italians would decide which side of the road they want to drive on! They tend to drive either in the middle, or on what I like to think of as 'my side', so that rearview mirrors are the first casualties of the journey. My nerves were the second.

The entire journey around the winding seaside road was accompanied by the blast of horns, wild waving of arms and the flashing of headlights. Just as I decided that I could only do the best I could do, a naked torso, black ponytail flying in the wind, roared past me on his motorbike swiping my left rear view mirror. At that moment I sighted another car roaring towards me— on my side of the road! Bill passed me the Ventolin to stave off an asthma attack from the stress. I swerved and he sped by us, shaking his fist in the air. I was so busy watching for enemy traffic that I hadn't been following the road signs.

We stopped to ask for directions in the first spot I could double park, while keeping an eye out for oncoming maniacs. Unfortunately, it seemed we were going the wrong way ... again! Someone had, comically they thought, turned the Positano sign around! I started to do a U-turn as a car pulled up on my tail and two motorbikes screeched to a halt in front of me. Bill hopped out to shout directions.

'Hard left, swing hard, harder, now straighten up, that's it, hard right, you can do it, keep going ...' He wasn't the only one shouting—but he was the only one I could understand!

Once we were heading in the right direction, the grandeur of the giant cliffs was breathtaking. The narrow ribbon of a road winds around the steep cliff face and the sheer drop to the aquamarine sea below is occasionally broken by a tiny brightly painted house clinging to the rock face.

Cars aren't suitable for the steep descent into Positano, so we parked at the first parking station halfway down the cliff. Our hotel, Buca di Bacco (the Caterpillars Hole) was at the foot of the cliff, right on the beachfront, so a young lad loaded us onto his cart, with me perched high on the front seat beside him and Bill crouching low, hanging half out the back.

We jolted downwards, klaxon horn blasting, hurtling down narrow winding alleyways just wide enough for us to squeeze through. I had two more puffs of ventolin and wondered if I would live long enough to enjoy another glass of wine.

Positano was originally a sleepy little fishing village situated opposite the Galli Islands, the legendary home of sirens who lured sailors to their doom. The hotels, bed and breakfasts and Moorish style homes cling to the cliff face, pretty pink, lemon and white buildings set in luxuriant gardens with crimson geraniums tumbling out of window boxes.

The tiny alleyways are lined with even tinier shops with goods spilling from hangers draped overhead. The narrow lanes are crowded with tourists from all over the world and the atmosphere is reminiscent of a festival. As the church bells rang, we strolled down to enjoy an Amaretto each in a cool vine-covered pergola at a café right on the beachfront. Nearby, an artist sketched while his dog snoozed in the sun. We watched the luxury yachts bobbing on the water and over the noisy families and laughing children we could just hear the waves lapping very gently against the sand.

Slim, tanned women in designer jeans and huge dark glasses sat with their just-as-elegant companions in designer T-shirts, jackets slung casually around their shoulders.

Dinner was on the candlelit terrace that overhangs the beach. I had risotto with baby spinach and gorgonzola and Bill worked his way through a very generous seafood platter. Our smiling waiter, Patrizio, and the sounds of music and laughter filtering up from the streets below, really made for a serene evening. It was balmy and even the stars seemed brighter than usual. Maybe it was just the romance of the place running away with me.

The next morning, breakfast was served on the terrace, where geraniums and petunias decorated the small round tables set with colourful tablecloths and fine china. Afterwards, we wandered in and out of the quaint shops that creep onto the sidewalks to buy our favourite *pane integrale*, *formaggio*, olives, *prosciutto cotto*, tiny stuffed mushrooms and marinated baby octopus, a string of vine-ripened tomatoes and some lush peaches—Bill had eventually relented to a picnic lunch.

We still had a bottle of a lovely Villa Branca wine and by lunchtime, passing couples laughed good-humouredly as we spread out our picnic blanket on a grassy verge. We toasted everyone who passed by, who in turn raised imaginary glasses to us. '*Salute*' and '*bravo*' they shouted enthusiastically, clearly bemused by our antics.

After our siesta we joined in the evening *passegiata*. Old ladies in long black dresses chattered in groups while the menfolk gathered in the bars and talked politics over limoncello.

Everyone greeted each other and even strangers paused to pat and admire the dogs pattering along on elaborately sequined leads. I like the way Italians dress up for *passegiata*—some of the older men wear hats and doff them as they nod '*Buona sera signora*'.

La Dolce Vita

Dainty icing-sugar-coated buns, hazelnut-covered chocolate sweets and crisp, toffee-topped desserts served with luscious homemade ice cream—it's no use resisting *la dolce vita* (the sweet life) in Italy.

Italian sweets are visual masterpieces, lovingly arranged on plates in grand displays of confectionery artwork. The variety and quality of *dolci* on offer is too hard to resist. They almost look too good to eat!

One of the earliest sweets Italians created was a doughy bread flavoured with honey and ricotta, called libum, initially used as a temple offering. It's also known as Cato's cheesecake, taking its name from the first-century Roman politician.

Sweets are flavoured with honey, candied fruit, nuts of all kinds, sweet spices, aniseed and often mascarpone, a thick Italian cream cheese.

Each region has its own favoured sweet, although a number of them originated in the south. Many of the desserts and cakes eaten from day-to-day are less sweet and far less elaborate.

In the south for instance, rice pudding flavoured with cinnamon is a simple pleasure. The north boasts the panettone, a cake eaten at Christmas time. Another popular sweet is the alcoholic, espresso-flavoured tiramisu (see page 25).

Libum

Carlo Zincone gave me this recipe for a sweet bread used as a temple offering in ancient times.

Makes 4

1 cup (4 oz) flour
8 oz ricotta cheese
1 egg, beaten
fresh bay leaves
½ cup (4 oz) clear honey

Preheat the oven to 425°F

Sift the flour into a bowl. Beat cheese in another bowl until soft and then add it to the flour, along with the egg. Knead into a soft dough and divide into four.

Mould each section into one round bun and place them all on a greased baking tray, placing one fresh bay leaf underneath each. Cover with foil and bake for 25 to 30 minutes until golden brown.

Warm the honey for a few seconds in a microwave oven and, when you remove the buns, score the top before pouring the warmed honey over them. Allow them to cool for 10 minutes before serving.

Frangelico chocolate cake
with raspberry sauce

Serves 8
200 g (6 oz) dark chocolate, chopped
100 g (3 oz) butter
5 eggs, separated
½ cup (4 oz) caster (superfine) sugar
⅓ cup (1½ oz) self-raising (self-rising) flour, sifted
½ cup (2 oz) hazelnuts, ground
¼ cup (2 fl oz) Frangelico liqueur

Raspberrry sauce
250 g (4 oz) fresh or frozen
125 raspberries
3 tablespoons icing (confectioners') sugar

Preheat oven to 190°C (375°F/Gas Mark 5).

Melt chocolate and butter over hot water, remove from heat and stir in egg yolks, sugar, flour, hazelnuts and Frangelico. Beat egg whites until soft peaks form.

Fold egg white lightly into chocolate mixture and pour into a greased and lined round 20 cm (8 in) springform cake tin and bake for 40–45 minutes, or until cake shrinks slightly from sides of tin.

To make the raspberry sauce, place raspberries and icing sugar in a food processor or blender and purée, until smooth. Strain, and add a little water if mixture is too thick.

Serve cake, cut into wedges, with raspberry sauce and extra cream.

Ice cream

Vanilla honey
3 cups thick cream
1 cup whole milk
½ cup honey
2 split vanilla beans,
(or 2 tablespoons of vanilla essence)
4 egg yolks

Slowly heat the cream, milk, honey and vanilla beans or the vanilla essence* in a saucepan, stirring from time to time until the mixture is hot and the sugar has been dissolved.

Put the four egg yolks in a bowl and whisk—at the same time slowly pour in about a cup of the hot liquid. Keep stirring until the mixture is smooth. Slowly pour this mixture into the remainder of the liquid in the saucepan, whisking constantly.

Keep stirring over a medium heat until the mixture thickens slightly and is able to coat the back of a spoon. This will probably take about 8 minutes but be careful not to let the mixture boil or it may curdle. Strain into a bowl and freeze in an ice cream machine or a tray in the deep freeze.

*Please note: If you use vanilla essence it's better to add this at the end, after straining.

Strawberry
2 punnets washed and hulled fresh strawberries
½ cup caster sugar
3 tablespoons fresh lemon juice
1½ cups thick cream

Puree the strawberries in a food processor. Stir in the remaining ingredients and then pour the mixture into an ice cream machine and freeze for about 20 minutes. If you don't have a machine, put in a tray in the deep freeze for longer period.
This recipe is also great with raspberries.

Ciao!

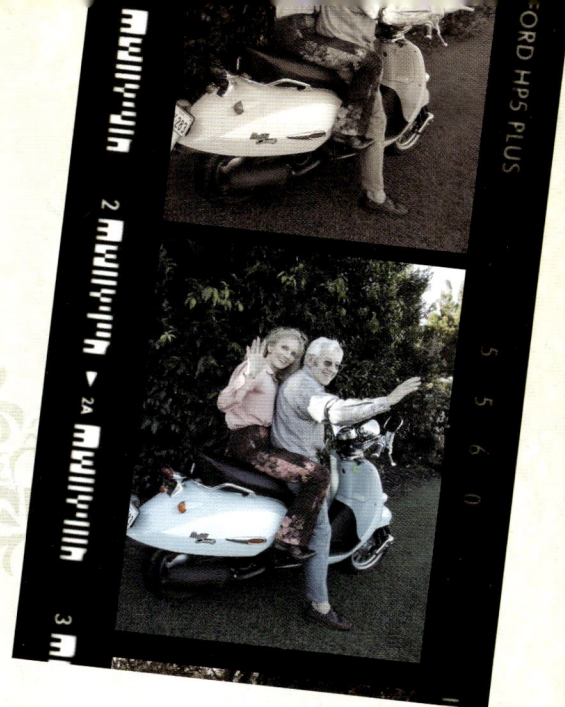

Bill here: I can't believe Patsy is actually letting me have the last word! *Ciao* is such a handy word—it means both hello and goodbye. It has universal meaning as a friendly greeting all over the world.

We enjoy Italy more with every visit, and even though my Italian isn't as good as Patsy's, I know enough for the essentials—I can order a beer and I can follow directions to the toilet!

I never cease to be astonished at the robust approach Italians have to life—their sheer pleasure in eating together is what makes every meal such an experience. Staying with Alvina and Umberto was a very special opportunity to see a side of Italy we'd never seen in other trips. We met people we wouldn't otherwise have met who invited us to share their meals, kept our glasses filled and made us feel very special.

Patsy's favourite memory was a picnic in a shady olive grove in San Gimignano, listening to the flautist, Andrea Cavallini, playing Vivaldi's *Sonata No 4*. It was a magical afternoon of delicious food, wine and music.

My favourite memory is of Positano—sitting in the afternoon sun waiting for Patsy (as usual), watching the boats bobbing up and down and remembering my sailing days. I watched a group of local fishermen at the table beside me playing cards, and before I knew it, they'd pulled up a chair, ordered an extra glass of wine and I was in the game! This outgoing warmth and friendliness is one of the things I miss most about Italy. That, and the way the Italians live and love amongst centuries old architecture, seemingly oblivious to their proud history.

We are already planning our next trip—this time to Sicily. We'll hire a car and after, becoming used to so many thousands of kilometres with Patsy at the wheel, I won't have to cover my eyes in horror as she swings out on to the 'wrong' side of the road when she's busy talking, (which is pretty much all of the time!)

The secret of successful travelling is going with the flow—not expecting it to be like it is at home, not expecting anything at all. Just discovering. I can never get enough of Italy! So even if it is sad to say *ciao*, I know that I'm really saying hello at the same time.

First published in Australia in 2006 by
New Holland Publishers (Australia) Pty Ltd
Sydney • Auckland • London • Cape Town

14 Aquatic Drive Frenchs Forest NSW 2086 Australia
218 Lake Road Northcote Auckland New Zealand
86 Edgware Road London W2 2EA United Kingdom
80 McKenzie Street Cape Town 8001 South Africa

National Library of Australia Cataloguing-in-Publication Data:

Rowe, Patsy.
   Irresistible Italy : a journey of the senses.

   ISBN 1 74110 353 3.

   1. Cookery, Italian. 2. Italy - Description and travel. I.
   Rowe, Bill. II. Title.

   914.5

Publisher: Fiona Schultz
Project Editor: Lliane Clarke
Designer: Tania Gomes
Production Manager: Linda Bottari
Printer: SNP/ Leefung Printing Co Ltd (China)

10 9 8 7 6 5 4 3 2 1